WHOLE BODY RESET

DIET COOKBOOK

Control your weight and muscle mass with delicious recipes
designed to get you the right amount of protein for meal | Reset
your body with a 30-day Smart Meal Plan

Dena Andrus

About the author

Writing a book can be the most challenging task only aspiring authors will complete it. With profound thinking, pursuing their vision and goals, sharpening their focus, respecting their time, and planning strategically, They are able to write such a masterpiece that brings revolutionary changes in the lives of people. Dena Andrus is one of them with a strong passion and desire to make a difference in people's lives as she shares an opinion that the world would be a happier, healthier, more human place if everyone follow the proper nutrition plan or instruction of a nutritionist.

Dena Andrus is a writer, nutritionist, recovery coach, and consultant who is dedicated to assisting others that a healthy diet is a crucial part of staying healthy and is essential for maintaining the body. In her books, She provides realistic and honest guidance so that their readers get the most out of reading her work. she shares her personal experience made on her skin, academic and independent studies as well as gives complete scientific backed information to help even ablute beginners benefit from her books.

Forty-three years Dena Andrus graduated in Nutrition and Dieting from a prestigious university. In her childhood, she was obese and grown-up bullied for her appearance, which became a sensitive spot for her. It made her feel humble about herself, and she wanted to turn her life around. And that's where proper nutrition come in which she experiences during her weight loss journey and wants her readers to learn from her experience.

Dena Andrus is also a mental coach as she believes that a mental approach is more important to losing weight. Her books will help the readers finally discover the most natural and efficient way for their bodies to lose weight without giving up the taste of the foods they love.

If you are looking to have more control over your health, let " Dena Andrus books" show the way.

Table of Contents

Introduction

Stephen Perrine creator and special projects editor for AARP the Magazine, where he oversees health and wellness coverage that reaches over 60 million readers, a popular dietary strategy for optimizing adaptive response to exercise. This strategy involves protein consumption before, during and after exercise. It can help with weight loss. However, it must be combined with a healthy diet to maintain a healthy weight and avoid nutrient deficiencies. Scheduling protein takes time and money if not done correctly. However, eating more protein every few hours has health benefits, including increased muscle mass. It could also reduce snacking on refined sugars between meals. A small study published in "Nutrition Research" found that skipping breakfast, eating more carbohydrates and snacking on high-sugar foods are linked to weight gain. But eating protein-rich meals every few hours has been linked to weight loss. The science behind protein timing. The timing of protein intake is important for athletic performance and body composition. Studies have shown that athletes improve muscle recovery and lean tissue preservation when they consume their last meal of the day very early in the evening.

In another study, a meal comprising 1.45 grams of protein every two hours was found to have a more profound effect on muscle protein turnover than those who eat at a slower rate of 0.8 grams per hour for six hours. Protein timing simply means planning your macronutrient intake to meet your needs at the most helpful time. If you want to lose fat, schedule your protein intake at breakfast or after your workout. Protein requires more calories to be broken down than it provides in return and is more satiating, which means you will be less likely to overeat when it is mealtime because you feel fuller (and therefore less likely to eat only junk food).

If you want to put on muscle, because of its role in the anabolic (muscle-building) process, the best thing to do is to make sure you are getting adequate protein at every meal. As for post-workout nutrition, research has shown that it's beneficial to take some protein before and after training.

The study on timing for fat loss was conducted by scientists at Laval University in Quebec City and was published in the Journal of Applied Physiology.

CHAPTER 1: What is Whole Body Reset Diet?

"Whole Body Reset Diet is a 15-day calorie-restricted diet. The plan is divided into three sections, five days each, most of the time spent drinking smoothies before transitioning back to regular meals. For instance, you will only consume smoothies during Phase One of the program. You will drink white smoothies in the morning, red smoothies for lunch, and green smoothies for dinner. White smoothies typically contain milk or Greek yogurt, excellent protein sources. Red smoothies are made of fruits and designed to give you more energy, and green smoothies are made of vegetables and keep you full throughout the night. In Phase Two, you will replace one of your smoothies with a salad, sandwich, or stir-fry and drink two smoothies daily. Finally, in Phase Three, a complete meal will place one of the two smoothies.

It is hypothesized that if a person consumes a low-calorie, plant-based diet for 15 days primarily composed of smoothies, they may train their body to use energy more effectively and burn calories faster, even while sleeping. In addition, by adding three days of strength training to your weekly routine, you will achieve long-term, healthy weight loss.

How does Whole Body Reset Diet work?

It does not allow you to "ease into" it. During your first five days on the plan, you'll be asked to do the following:

- White, red, and green smoothies replace breakfast, lunch, and dinner.
- Each day, you should consume two crunchy snacks that range from 150 to 200 calories, such as a ¼ cup of edamame.
- Every day, walk at least 10,000 steps.
- Plan on performing at least five minutes of weight training at least five days a week. Some examples of resistance training include a circuit of 20 reverse flies, dips, planks, and hamstring curls.

CHAPTER 2: How to Follow Whole Body Reset Diet

Alternate between smoothies, crunchy snacks, and meals for 15 days. Fiber consumption is stressed in this diet because fiber is low in calories. This helps keep you full while maintaining healthy digestion and a healthy metabolism. Here's what to expect:

- For each meal, stick to the dietary guidelines.
- Build each dish around the same ingredient categories.
- Food preparation should take no more than five minutes.

Avoid foods that are rich in fat or calories, such as:

- Fried food and junk food
- Refined grains
- Alcohol
- Processed meat
- Soda
- Candy

Here's a deeper look at each step to help determine if this diet is for you.

Smoothie Phase (Days 1-5)

The smoothie phase is the reset phase, and there is no gradual introduction to the diet. For most people, this is a significant change.

The regimen begins with a solid-food cleanse, followed by three smoothies daily.

- Protein-rich ingredients like yogurt are used in a white morning smoothie
- Fruit is in the red lunch smoothie
- Smoothie with veggies for dinner

You will also have two "crunchy" snacks high in protein and fiber to keep you feeling full throughout the day. The first stage of the sample menu is as follows:

- Green goddess smoothie for breakfast
- Kalamata olive tapenade as a snack
- Avocado-lime smoothie for lunch
- Walnut bites as a snack
- Broccoli carrot lettuce smoothie for dinner

Phase Two (Days 6-10)

In Phase Two, you add an exercise regimen and one "S" meal each day during this phase. Salad, stir fry, sandwich, and soup are examples of "S" meals. You will not overeat if you eat a one-item meal. One smoothie will be replaced with an "S" meal. It doesn't matter which smoothie you skip if you incorporate it into your daily diet. For example, substitute veggies for supper if you don't have the green smoothie.

Phase Two of the sample menu

- Celery dill soup for breakfast
- Tomatoes deviled eggs as a snack
- Mango smoothie for lunch
- Yogurt parfait as a snack
- A Berry banana lettuce Smoothie for dinner

Final Phase (Days 10-15)

During the final phase, you'll swap two smoothies for an "S" meal. You'll also engage in more physical activity. Once the diet is finished, this phase will help you transition to a healthy lifestyle.

Phase Three of the sample menu

- American pancakes for breakfast
- Coffee walnut bars as a snack
- Ginger sesame pork soup for lunch
- Chocolate protein muffins as a snack
- Protein-rich oatmeal for dinner

After Completing the Diet

After you've finished, you'll use the same ideas to incorporate healthy behaviors into your everyday routine.

You may customize your plan to meet your lifestyle, but it should include the following items:

- Every day, there are five meals (one smoothie, two snacks, and two solid meals)
- Free meals are provided twice a week
- Strive for 10,000 steps per day and 10 minutes of weight exercise at least three times per week

Exercise

To begin the diet, avoiding strenuous activity and focusing on low-impact exercises is advisable. On the other hand, you should walk at least 10,000 steps every day.

During Phase Two of the program, you should complete a home workout lasting five minutes three times per week. Additionally, yoga and Pilates are options. Rather than exercising, the goal is to tone your physique.

The following five days should be spent concentrating on body strengthening. Throughout the day, alternate between two 5-minute resistance training circuits. Following the diet, you can resume your regular exercise program as long as it includes some weight training and everyday walking.

CHAPTER 3: Whole Body Reset Diet practical guidelines

Whole Body Reset Diet is a 5-step protocol you follow over 15 days. For those 15 days, you will choose a dietary approach best suited to your lifestyle and schedule. The diet removes foods and beverages that cause stress, irritate the digestive system, or or are hard to cook or find.

How this works:

- As much as possible, avoid eating food after 7 pm daily until the next day's breakfast time, only starting the day with a fast the next morning.
- Avoid restaurants or cafeterias and processed foods such as bread, cake, cookies, sweets, and snack foods.
- Always keep protein powder with you or compare other food options to see which are least tempting. Your primary goal will be to go three whole days without eating.
- It's vital to consume plenty of water, specifically alkaline. If you feel hungry, try having a cup of organic vegetable juice or mineral water.

You will need to plan and prepare your food the night before. Day one, eat until full. Then, when you feel physically satiated, stop eating. The diet's focus is to reset your body's system, which includes getting rid of "stressors" from digestion, hormones, blood sugar regulation, and brain chemistry contributing to weight gain or slow metabolism. The diet is a means for re-training your body's self-regulatory system; it also gives you a chance to detoxify from the food items you may have been consuming daily.

Importance of taking fluids 2 to 3 hours before meals

It is recommended that we drink fluids 2 to 3 hours before eating. Water or other liquids too close to meals can dilute digestive enzymes and stomach acid, impeding digestion and leading to indigestion. In addition, too much water may fill us up and make us less hungry for our meals.

You probably notice this yourself when you drink water before meals. When we take in liquids just before or with a meal, we tend to eat less at that meal and sometimes skip the next one. Therefore, drinking liquids before a meal is like eating and drinking simultaneously, slowing digestion.
Drinking too close to meals is not a good idea because we lose body heat from our mouths when we drink cold liquids. If you are thirsty, try alternating over a few meals between sipping room temperature and iced liquid, so your stomach does not become accustomed at once. If you like cold drinks, try to drink liquids nice and slowly.

Drinking water before meals is fine, but do not drink juices or milk after meals. These drinks contain more sugar than plain water and can sometimes make you feel bloated. For example, fruit juices are very high in sugar for a specific reason. Fruit contains fructose (fruit sugar) and glucose (table sugar). To get the fruit's sugar into our bodies, it must be broken down by the digestive system.
In nature, animals that eat fruit must either eat the whole fruit or wait for it to ferment to create alcohol because the body cannot absorb the sugar in its natural state. Humans, on the other hand, can easily absorb sugar. That is why fresh juice tastes better than most bottled juice beverages.

Another reason fresh fruit is better than fruit juice is the storage of fresh fruit contains many microorganisms that can spoil the juice. In addition, juice containing a high amount of sugar has not been pasteurized, so it contains more bacteria that can cause us to get sick. Avoid all drinks after meals, including milk, juice, and yogurt.

How much fluid should we drink before meals? Many people drink while cooking and after meals. Of course, you can drink plain water if it goes down easily and you don't feel bloated. If you consume any other liquids before or after meals, try to limit yourself to not more than a third cup before a meal and the same amount with each meal.

If you are someone who cannot wait until you have finished your meal to enjoy a beverage, remember that it is still beneficial to finish your meals before consuming the beverage. For example, finish lunch before having a lemonade if you crave a drink with your lunch.

Do not drink liquids with meals if that interferes with enjoying your food. If you find yourself eating more slowly, chewing more often, and feeling more satisfied after meals, you can be confident that your digestive system is working optimally.

Differences between white, red, and green smoothies

Which smoothie color is the best? Most people prefer red or green, but what are the differences between both? Read on to find out!

Green smoothies typically contain more leafy greens such as spinach and kale, while reds incorporate beets into their ingredients. And according to many nutritionists and professional athletes, white smoothies often provide more nutrients than other drinks.

Ingredients like red beets, carrots, celery, and other fruits and vegetables are frequently found in red smoothies. This is because beets have a high concentration of nitrates, which, when metabolized by the body, become nitric oxide and aid in the relaxation of blood vessels. Beets are responsible for this effect. This can help you give you an amazing, positive boost in your energy levels.

White smoothies may contain all kinds of ingredients depending on the person, but some of the most common are spinach, blueberries, cucumbers, and walnuts. The health advantages of white smoothies are frequently attributed to their antioxidants and anti-inflammatory characteristics. These properties lower the chance of developing chronic diseases such as cancer and cardiovascular diseases.

Red smoothies are rich in anthocyanins, which can help lower homocysteine levels in the blood, a marker for heart disease. In addition, reds are also high in vitamins A and C, which help boost your immune system. This can be especially beneficial if you're going through a "cold" season.

Green smoothies are the healthiest, containing all the vitamins and minerals you want in your daily diet. They also have high amounts of antioxidants, proven to positively affect your skin, hair, and nails. Many recipes use fresh ingredients like raw spinach and kale, which taste delicious and help make you healthier.

A red smoothie can provide you with many health benefits as well. This is because reds are packed with anthocyanins, an antioxidant proven to help lower inflammation and boost your cardiovascular system.

Every smoothie will contain fruit, but there are a few differences between the types. Some smoothies contain all fruits (green, red, and white), varying their nutritional value depending on the fruit included. For example, red smoothies include beets, carrots, and apples, which have a higher concentration of nitrates than other ingredients.

Blueberries, bananas, and strawberries are all common ingredients in green smoothies due to their high nutrient content. They contain a lot of fiber and can help boost your immune system.

White smoothies are typically a few ingredients, such as cucumber, spinach, blueberries, and blackberries. As you can see, the main difference between each drink is the color of the ingredients included.

You can get many benefits from drinking a red or green smoothie daily. Drinking a green smoothie is recommended because it contains plenty of antioxidants. Antioxidants are natural substances that can help stop free radicals from harming your body. Free radicals are dangerous molecules that can damage cells and increase your risk of developing cancer and heart disease.

Red smoothies, on the other hand, are packed with antioxidants and nitrates, reducing inflammation and improving cardiovascular health.

Green smoothies are high in vitamin C, essential for your immune system. In addition, they contain vitamins A and E that can help fight free radicals that play a role in increasing the risk of cancer. Green smoothies are also rich in fiber and water, providing energy and keeping you hydrated throughout the day. These smoothies often have a thicker consistency and different textures depending on the ingredients used.

Red smoothies are often smooth and creamy, similar to yogurt. They also contain high amounts of antioxidants which can help reduce the risk of many health problems. These smoothies typically do not have as much fiber as green smoothies and are usually sweeter, making them easier to drink daily.

While white smoothies may be very convenient, as they only take a few minutes to prepare, you don't get the same benefits as drinking green, red, or blue smoothies. However, if you have time to prepare a green or red smoothie regularly, then you should do so. Because of the high levels of antioxidants in certain beverages, drinking them can benefit your general health.

When considering your daily health, it's essential to know that drinking a white smoothie can be beneficial from time to time. While it may not provide the same benefits as other smoothies, it is high in fiber and water, boosting your energy levels and keeping you hydrated for the entire day.

CHAPTER 4: Benefits of the Whole-Body Reset

Although Whole Body Reset Diet has not been scientifically validated, some of its core principles have. Here are some of the diet's potential benefits:

Assist You in Losing Weight

People will almost immediately see weight loss success with Whole Body Reset Diet. Losing weight comes down to burning more calories than you take in through food and drink. Your body will most likely be in a calorie deficit because this method comprises low-calorie smoothies, snacks, and meals. The exercise routine included in the plan also aids in calorie burning.

To put it in context, this diet delivers roughly 1,200–1,400 calories per day, significantly less than the 2,000 calories required for normal adults to maintain their weight. Dieters on a comparable 1,200–1,400-calorie diet consisting of two meals and two meal replacement smoothies per day dropped 15 pounds (6.8 kg) on average in one trial.

This was, however, throughout a one-year weight-loss and maintenance program. It's also crucial to remember that weight reduction is influenced by various characteristics, including age, weight, height, and sex.

Keep You Motivated

Even though 15 days is short, whatever weight you lose during this time may inspire you to continue with Whole Body Reset Diet. This is because quick weight loss, in the beginning, has been linked to long-term diet success.

On the other hand, low early weight loss is linked to increased weight loss program dropout rates. This disparity could be attributable to motivation levels, according to researchers. Those who see rapid results are more likely to stick with the program because they believe it is effective.

Provides Highly Nutritious Foods

Foods including fruits, vegetables, legumes, nuts, whole grains, low-fat dairy, and lean protein are all included in Whole Body Reset Diet. These foods include a wide range of essential nutrients, making them an important part of a balanced diet. Foods rich in fibre are also included in the smoothies, snacks, and dinners in Whole Body Reset Diet meal plan. Type-2 diabetes, cardiovascular disease, cancer, and other chronic diseases are less likely to develop in people who eat diets high in fibre.

CHAPTER 5: Foods to Eat

Whole Body Reset Diet requires that you consume food five times daily. It offers low-calorie smoothies, snacks, and dinners as part of its meal plan.

Smoothies

Smoothies are served three times daily during Phase 1, twice daily during Phase 2, and once daily during Phase 3.

Though Perrine does not specify a serving size for the smoothies, he provides a 270–325 calorie range per smoothie.

Nonetheless, if you weigh more than 175 pounds (79 kg), you may raise serving sizes by one-third to accommodate higher calorie and nutritional requirements.

Smoothies are produced using four primary components, the ingredients of which can be substituted according to personal preference:

- **Liquid base:** flavored water, water, low or nonfat milk, or non-dairy milk like almond or soy milk
- **Protein:** tofu, protein powder, or fat-free yogurt
- **Healthy fat:** nuts, avocado, or seeds

- **High fiber carbs:** Oranges, berries, apples, pears, and leafy green vegetables like spinach or kale, are recommended for their fiber content.

Sweeteners are not permitted in the smoothies, including cane sugar, honey, maple syrup, and packaged fruits with additional sweeteners.

There are three sorts of smoothie recipes: white, red, and green smoothies, which are called by the colors they produce when combined.

Snacks

You eat low-calorie snacks twice a day during the whole 15-day diet.

Each snack should have about 150 calories, be low in sugar, and contain at least 5 grams of protein and fiber.

Examples of:
- edamame
- air-popped popcorn
- celery with a dollop of peanut butter
- fat-free cheese on healthy wheat crackers
- deli turkey slices with apple slices

Meals

Phases 2 and 3 include the addition of homemade solid meals. To assist you, the book contains dishes that range in calories from 230 to 565 for each single-dish meal.

The dishes use natural, minimally processed ingredients and have a healthy mix of protein, fiber, and fats. Several examples include the following:

- **Salads:** lush greens topped with chopped vegetables, fruit, nuts, and a lean protein source such as lentils or chicken, served with a homemade olive oil dressing
- **Sandwiches:** whole grain bread, deli meat, vegetables, and low-fat condiments or cheese
- **Soups:** prepared with low-sodium broth, veggies, spices, and lean protein sources such as lentils or chicken breast and served with whole-grain bread.
- **Stir-fries:** lean protein sources such as chicken breast or shrimp are combined with veggies, spices, brown rice, or soba noodles.
- Scrambled egg whites with vegetables, low-fat cheese, spices, and high-fiber carbohydrates such as whole-grain bread or potatoes.

Only calorie-free drinks are allowed, including water, flavored water, unsweetened coffee, and unsweetened tea.

CHAPTER 6: Foods to Avoid

Because Whole Body Reset Diet is based on a predetermined food plan with recipes, there is little space for deviation.

You should always avoid the following items throughout the first 15 days of the diet:

- cheese, full-fat milk, and yogurt
- fried or overly processed meals
- pasta, white bread, and other refined grains
- other sugary beverages and soda
- alcohol

Perrine's justification is that whole milk and processed meals are heavy in saturated fats, traditionally considered harmful. However, some scientific research shows that the fats included in full-fat dairy products do not hurt — and may even benefit — heart health (24Trusted Source).

Refined grains are prohibited because they have a high glycemic index (GI), a metric indicating how rapidly blood sugar levels rise in response to eating (25Trusted Source).

Additionally, alcohol is not permitted during the first 15 days because of its high-calorie content. Perrine further believes that drunkenness impairs your capacity to burn fat and may result in bad dietary choices.

CHAPTER 7: Tips to Succeed with Whole Body Reset Diet

A "whole-body reset" diet involves a lot of discipline. It requires a lot of planning and preparation, but if you are committed to success, the weight loss will be well worth it. Here are some tips to help you along the way:

- Follow the 15-day diet plan with 3 phases. You will be able to easily acclimatize to the new diet this way.
- Make a day of it by planning your meals. Make sure you're prepared in case you get hungry or crave something you shouldn't.
- Also, make sure to get enough rest. This will help you feel less hungry and give you more energy throughout the day.
- Be prepared for a lot of exercise during these 15 days. You will have to do 5- to 10-minute resistance workout sessions to burn fat and build muscle.
- Be sure to drink plenty of water. If you are not accustomed to drinking a lot of water, start with 1 gallon per day and gradually increase the amount as you need it.

- If you do not have a membership to a gym, you can work out at home using free weights or by purchasing an exercise ball.
- Get plenty of support from family members and friends while trying this diet out. They can encourage you when you're feeling discouraged by not being able to stick with it long enough, or they can cheer you on when your efforts seem worth it!

The diet is strict, so it may be challenging to stick with 15 days. However, it's essential to remember that this is a lifestyle shift. You won't be able to stay on your diet forever, but you will be able to see results and feel better about yourself for having tried it!

CHAPTER 8: Phase One

Shopping List

Fruits

Strawberries

Nectarine

Banana

Blueberries

Mango

Watermelon

Raspberries

Blackberries

Avocado

Dairy

Coconut milk

Coconut butter

Unsweetened almond milk

Whipping cream

Peanut butter

Whey protein

Vanilla Greek yogurt

Eggs

Mayonnaise

Butter

Vegetables

Kale

Parsley

Purple cabbage

Celery

Chives

Roma tomatoes

Dandelion greens

Romaine lettuce

Spinach

Cucumber

Basil

Brussels sprouts

Broccoli

Carrot

Green pepper

Zucchini

Yellow onion

Potatoes

Baby Bella mushrooms

Fresh oregano

White onion

Oils

Coconut oil

Olive oil

Extra virgin rapeseed oil

Extra virgin oil

Baking staples

Almond flour

Almond extract

Egg white protein powder

Vanilla extract

Lemon extract

Coconut flour

Granulated sweetener

Vanilla

Baking powder

Eggs

Dry

Dark chocolate

Vanilla protein powder

Plain protein powder

Green tea powder

Sugar

Almonds

Pumpkin seeds

Sunflower seeds

Raw peanuts

Bay leaves

Unsweetened coconut flakes

Coffee

Walnut

Chia seeds

Others

Pitted Kalamata olives

Cloves garlic

Capers

Mint Sprigs

Lemon zest

Granola

Low-carb beer

Ice

Cider vinegar

Balsamic vinegar

sweet paprika

unsweetened coconut flesh

Stevia

Lime

Purified water

freshly grated ginger

Vegetable stock

Silken tofu

low-sodium, fat-free chicken broth

Seasoning

Cajun seasoning

Salt

Pepper

Barbecue dry rub seasoning

Hot sauce

Kosher salt

Cracked black pepper

Hot red pepper sauce

WHITE SMOOTHIES

Strawberry and Coconut Smoothie

For persons weighing 77kg and over, increase the ingredients by one-third.

Preparation Time: 5 Mins

Cooking Time: 0 Mins

Serving: 2

Ingredients

- 2 cups of frozen strawberries
- 1 cup coconut milk
- 1 tbsp coconut butter
- 1 nectarine, sliced

Directions

1. Put the ingredients into a blender with a high-powered motor and process until smooth.

2. Transfer to your glasses, then serve and enjoy!

Nutrition

Calories: 262 | Carbs: 50g | Fat: 7g | Protein: 3g

Almond Kale Smoothie

For persons weighing 77kg and over, increase the ingredients by one-third.

Preparation Time: 5 Mins

Cooking Time: 0 Mins

Servings: 2

Ingredients

- 1 cup crushed ice
- 1 cup unsweetened almond milk
- 1 cup kale
- 1 tbsp coconut oil
- 2 tbsp almond flour
- ½ tbsp almond extract

Directions

1. In a blender, combine a half cup of ice, almond milk, kale, and coconut oil.

2. Stir in the remaining half cup of ice, almond flour, and almond extract. Serve immediately after 1 minute of blending, or until smooth.

Nutrition

Calories: 350 | Fat: 39g | Protein: 4g | Carbs: 7g

Lemon High Protein Smoothie

For persons weighing 77 kg and over, increase the ingredients by one-third.

Preparation Time: 5 Mins

Cooking Time: 0 Mins

Servings: 2

Ingredients

- 1 cup unsweetened almond milk
- ½ coconut milk
- 2 tbsp egg white protein powder

- 1 tbsp pure vanilla extract
- 1 tsp lemon extract
- 2 cups ice cubes

Directions

1. In a blender, blend the almond milk, coconut milk, egg white powder, vanilla, plus lemon extract, until combined.

2. After adding the ice, blend the mixture until it is smooth and thick, and serve.

Nutrition

Calories: 372 | Fat: 14g | Protein: 6g | Carbs: 3g

Green Tea Smoothie

For persons weighing 77kg and over, increase the ingredients by one-third.

Preparation Time: 5 Mins

Cooking Time: 0 Mins

Servings: 2

Ingredients

- 1 cup crushed ice
- 1 cup unsweetened almond milk
- ¼ cup heavy (scourging) cream
- 1 tbsp coconut oil
- 3 tbsp unsweetened vanilla protein powder
- ½ tbsp green tea powder

Directions

1. Blend together in a blender a portion of a cup of ice, a portion of a cup of almond milk, a portion of heavy cream, and a portion of coconut oil.

2. After the half cup of ice has been added, the vanilla protein powder and the green tea protein powder can be added to the shake or smoothie.

3. Blend for one minute, or until a smooth consistency is reached.

Nutrition

Calories: 310 | Fat: 41g | Protein: 17g | Carbs: 4g

Choco Banana Smoothie

For persons weighing 77 kg and over, increase the ingredients by one-third.

Preparation Time: 5 minutes

Cooking Time: 0 minutes

Servings: 2

Ingredients

- ½ cup almond milk
- 1 tbsp peanut butter
- ¼ frozen banana
- ½ scoop whey protein (chocolate)

Directions

1. Use a blender to fully combine the ingredients until you get the desired consistency.

2. "Pour into a glass and enjoy."

Nutrition

Calories: 298 | Carbs: 25g | Fat: 16g | Protein: 18g

SNACKS

Kalamata Olive Tapenade

For persons weighing 77 kg and over, increase the ingredients by one-third.

Preparation Time: 15 minutes
Cooking Time: 0 minutes
Servings: 8
Ingredients

- 1 cup of pitted Kalamata olives
- 3 peeled cloves of garlic
- 2 tbsp capers
- 2 tbsp lemon juice
- 3 tbsp chopped fresh parsley
- Salt and to taste
- 2 tbsp olive oil

Directions

1. Place the garlic cloves in the container of a blender and give them a few short pulses in order to mince them.

2. To the mixture, add the olive oil, capers, olives, and parsley. Follow up with the lemon juice.

3. Continue to blend until everything is in little pieces.

4. Pepper and salt can be used to season the dish according to personal preference.

Nutrition

81 Calories | Protein 0.5g | Carbohydrates 2.5g | Fat 7.9g | Sodium 359.3mg

Yogurt Parfait

For persons weighing 77 kg and over, increase the ingredients by one-third.

Preparation Time: 10 mins
Cooking Time: 0 mins
Servings: 2
Ingredients

- ½ cup of fresh strawberries, diced
- 1 tbsp lemon zest
- ½ cup of fresh blueberries
- 1 tbsp white sugar
- 1- 6 oz container nonfat vanilla Greek yogurt
- 6 tbsp granola, or as required

Directions

1. Put the blueberries and strawberries in a bowl and mix. Sugar should be sprinkled over the berries before they are mixed.

2. Put two tablespoons of granola into the bottom of each parfait glass. Place 2 tablespoons of yogurt on top, then dust with a half teaspoon of lemon zest. Finally, place a third of the berries on top. Continue layering

the ingredients until the parfait glasses are full.

3. Repeat steps 1 and 2 to the rim of each parfait glass.

Nutrition

264 Calories | Protein 9g | Carbohydrates 26.2g | Fat 14.1g | Sodium 61.2mg

Dark Chocolate and Almond Bark

For persons weighing 77 kg and over, increase the ingredients by one-third.

Preparation Time: 20 Mins

Cooking Time: 10 Mins

Servings: 8 barks

Ingredients

- 7 oz dark chocolate (at least 75% cocoa)
- 3-½ oz almonds
- 2 oz pumpkin seeds
- 2 oz sunflower seeds

Directions

1. Put parchment paper on a baking sheet and set it aside.

2. Throw away any chocolate bits that are too large, then place the smaller pieces in a container that can withstand high temperatures. Put the dish you want to boil on top of the container that contains the bubbling water, and then let it there for a couple of minutes.

3. Allow the chocolate to melt in a simmering saucepan, stirring occasionally.

4. As soon as half of the chocolate has liquefied, eliminate the heat-resilient dish and set it aside to calm.

5. When the chocolate has cooled down but is still warm, stir in the almonds, pumpkin seeds, and sunflower seeds.

6. Spread the chocolate across the lined tray and smooth the top to be even. Place in the fridge for 10 to 15 minutes to harden.

7. Once hardened, cut the bark into 8 servings, and relish!

Nutrition

Calories 156 | Carbs 12g | Protein 16g | Fat 17g

Slow-Cooked Cajun Boiled Peanuts

For persons weighing 77 kg and over, increase the ingredients by one-third.

Preparation Time: 5 minutes

Cooking Time: 12 hours

Servings: 6 cups

Ingredients

- 6 cups uncooked peanuts in the shell
- 2- 12 oz bottles or cans of low-carb beer
- 4 cups water
- 2 tbsp Cajun seasoning
- 4 bay leaves

Directions

1. Combine the peanuts, beer, water, and Cajun seasoning with the bay leaves on the stove.

2. Cook for a maximum of 12 hours on high with the lid on.

3. Remove any excess liquid from the peanuts, then set them aside to cool for 10 minutes.

4. As you munch, enjoy the peanuts and toss the shells; then, place any leftovers in a jar that seals tightly and store them in the fridge.

Nutrition

Calories: 153 | Fat: 14g | Carbs: 3g | Protein: 7g

Deviled Tomatoes

For persons weighing 77 kg and over, increase the ingredients by one-third.

Preparation Time: 15 Mins

Cooking Time: 0 Mins

Servings: 4-6

Ingredients

- 6 large hardboiled eggs, skinned and roughly chopped
- ¼ cup chopped celery
- ¼ cup sliced fresh chives, plus extra to garnish
- 2 tbsp mayonnaise
- 2 tbsp Creole or grainy mustard
- 4 dashes of hot sauce
- 1 tsp barbecue dry rub seasoning
- ¼ tsp kosher salt
- ½ tsp splintered black pepper
- 6 small Roma tomatoes
- ½ cup finely carved purple cabbage

Directions

1. Using a mixer or big bowl, thoroughly blend the chopped egg yolks and celery and chives in the mayonnaise mixture, followed by the remaining ingredients.

2. Cover and refrigerate while you prep the tomatoes.

3. Using a spoon, scoop out the seeds and pulp from each Roma tomato half lengthwise.

4. Scoop 1 to 2 tablespoons of the egg mixture into each tomato half. Garnish with chives and slices of purple cabbage.

Nutrition

Calories: 152 | Fat: 11g | Carbs: 9g | Protein: 11g

RED SMOOTHIES

Mango Smoothie

For persons weighing 77 kg and over, increase the ingredients by one-third.

Preparation Time: 5 Mins

Cooking Time: 0 Mins

Servings: 3-4

Ingredients

- ½ dandelion greens
- ½ romaine lettuce
- 2 mangos, skinned and pit detached
- 1 banana, skinned
- ½ purified water

Directions

1. In a blender, thoroughly purée the dandelion greens, romaine lettuce, mangoes, bananas, and half of the water.

2. While the mixture is being blended, gradually add the remaining water until the appropriate consistency is reached.

Nutrition

Calories: 276 | Fat: 1g | Protein: 1g | Carbs: 34g

Watermelon Banana Smoothie

For persons weighing 77 kg and over, increase the ingredients by one-third.

Preparation Time: 5 Mins

Cooking Time: 0 Mins

Servings: 3

Ingredients

- 2 cups watermelon
- 1 banana, peeled
- 1 cup coconut milk
- 1 cup ice

Directions

1. Blend the watermelon, banana, and coconut milk in a blender with a half cup of ice until everything is fully blended.

2. While the mixture is being blended, gradually add the remaining ice until the required consistency is reached.

Nutrition

Calories: 274 | Fat: 16g | Protein: 3g | Carbs: 19g

Spinach-Blueberry Smoothie

For persons weighing 77 kg and over, increase the ingredients by one-third.

Preparation Time: 5 Mins

Cooking Time: 0 Mins

Servings: 2

Ingredients

- 1 cup coconut milk

- 1 cup spinach
- ½ English cucumber, severed
- ½ cup blueberries
- 1 scoop plain protein powder
- 2 tbsp coconut oil
- 4 ice cubes
- Mint sprigs for garnish

Directions

1. Put the ice, spinach, and cucumber into the blender, along with the blueberries, protein powder, and coconut oil, and process all of the ingredients until you have a creamy consistency.

2. After that, finish by assisting with the mint, which acts as an enhancer.

Nutrition

Calories: 323 | Fat: 32g | Protein: 15g | Carbs: 6g

Coconut Berry Smoothie

For persons weighing 77 kg and over, increase the ingredients by one-third.

Preparation Time: 5 Mins

Cooking Time: 0 Mins

Servings: 2

Ingredients

- 1 cup smashed ice, divided
- 1 cup unsweetened coconut milk
- 1 tbsp coconut oil
- ½ cup raspberries
- ½ cup blackberries
- 2 tbsp unsweetened coconut shavings

Directions

1. Put a half cup of ice, some coconut milk, and some coconut oil into a blender.

2. Blend until smooth. Blend to a smooth consistency.

3. Add the remaining half cup of ice, the berries, and the coconut shavings to the blender and pulse until everything is combined.

4. Blend to a smooth consistency.

5. After blending to a smooth consistency, serve.

Nutrition

Calories: 320 | Fat: 38g | Protein: 4g | Carbs: 8g

Avocado Blueberry Smoothie

For persons weighing 77 kg and over, increase the ingredients by one-third.

Preparation Time: 5 Mins

Cooking Time: 0 Mins

Servings: 2

Ingredients

- 1 cup smashed ice, divided
- ½ cup blueberries
- ¾ cup unsweetened almond milk
- 2 tbsp heavy (whipping) cream
- 1 tbsp coconut oil
- 1 avocado, skinned and crushed

Directions

1. You may make this smoothie by using an ice cube tray and some blueberries.

2. You can also use almond milk, heavy emulsion, and one tbsp of coconut oil.

3. Blend the avocado with the remaining ice cubes in a blender.

4. Blend until smooth, about a minute.

5. Drink.

Nutrition

Calories: 325 | Fat: 54g | Protein: 1g | Carbs: 1g

SNACKS 2

Coffee Walnut Bars

For persons weighing 77 kg and over, increase the ingredients by one-third.

Preparation Time: 15 minutes

Cooking Time: 15 minutes

Servings: 14 bars

Ingredients

- 110g butter, melted
- 125ml coffee
- 60g coconut flour
- 55g walnuts, chopped
- 8 eggs
- 1 tsp baking powder
- 2 tsp vanilla
- 5 tbsp granulated sweetener
- A pinch of salt

Directions

1. In a container, combine the butter, vanilla extract, and sweetener.

2. A dash of salt, baking powder, coconut flour, and coffee should be added to the batter. Stir thoroughly.

3. Mix thoroughly after adding each egg one at a time.

4. Mix in the walnuts that have been chopped.

5. After pouring the mixture onto a sweltering dish creased with baking paper, place it in the kiln at 356°F for 15 minutes.

6. After it has cooled, cut it into 14 separate bars.

Nutrition

Calories: 150 | Fat: 11g | Carbs: 3g | Protein: 4g

Basil & Olive Eggs

For persons weighing 77kg and over, increase the ingredients by one-third.

Preparation Time: 15 Mins

Cooking Time: 0 Mins

Servings: 3

Ingredients

- 3 large eggs
- 6 pitted Kalamata olives
- 1 handful basil
- 1 tsp cider vinegar
- 1 tbsp extra virgin rapeseed oil

Directions

1. Boil the eggs and transfer them into cold water. Peel and halve, then scoop out the yolks.

2. Put the vinegar, oil, basil, and oil in a bowl. Season it with pepper, and then use a hand blender to blitz the ingredients. Mix everything thoroughly before adding the egg yolk.

3. Place the mixture in the eggs using a spoon, then place them in the refrigerator to chill.

Nutrition

Calories: 157 | Carbs: 1g | Fat: 11g | Protein: 10g

Oven-Roasted Brussels Sprouts

For persons weighing 77 kg and over, increase the ingredients by one-third.

Preparation Time: 10 minutes

Cooking Time: 15-20 minutes

Servings: 4

Ingredients

- 1 lb brussels sprouts, clipped and shared
- 3 tbsp extra-virgin olive oil
- Sea salt, as needed
- Freshly pulverized black pepper, as needed
- 1-½ tbsp balsamic vinegar

Directions

1. Turn the oven temperature up to 375°F.

2. Give the brussels sprouts a quick toss in the oil. Arrange them on a rimmed baking sheet in a single layer with the cut sides facing down. Add little salt and pepper before serving.

3. To get the best results, bake the baking plate for fifteen minutes in the kiln. Once the balsamic vinegar has been sprinkled over the sprouts, toss them with the vinegar and set aside.

4. The vinegar should have caramelised, but not burned, by the time you place your baking pan back into the kiln. After cooking, serve immediately.

Nutrition

Calories: 150 | Fat: 11g | Carbs: 10g | Protein: 5g

Nuts and Seed Bowls

For persons weighing 77kg and over, increase the ingredients by one-third.

Preparation Time: 5 Mins

Cooking Time: 20 Mins

Servings: 6

Ingredients

- 1 cup of walnuts
- 1 cup almonds
- 1 tbsp sunflower seeds
- 2 tbsp olive oil
- A touch of salt and black pepper
- ½ tsp sweetened paprika

Directions

1. In a dish, add the walnuts, almonds, and seeds with the remaining elements; then, spread it out on a baking pan that has been prepared with parchment paper.

2. After baking for 20 minutes at 400°F, the mixture is poured into dishes and offered as a snack.

Nutrition

Calories 150g | Fat 2g | Carbs 5g | Protein 5g

Coconut Squares

For persons weighing 77 kg and over, increase the ingredients by one-third.

Preparation Time: 10 Mins

Cooking Time: 30 Mins

Servings: 8

Ingredients

- 2 cups coconut flour
- 1 cup coconut flesh, unsweetened and shredded
- 1 cup of walnuts, chopped
- 1 cup coconut oil
- ¼ tsp Stevia
- Cooking spray

Directions

1. Flour, coconut flesh, and the other ingredients, excluding the cooking spray, should be mixed together in a basin and thoroughly stirred before proceeding.

2. Put this into a baking dish that has been sprayed with cooking spray. Press it down firmly on the bottom, then put it into a kiln pre-heated to 350°F and bake it for 30 minutes.

3. Put to the side so it can cool, then equally cut it into squares and serve.

Nutrition

Calories 300 | Fat 13.4g | Carbs 6.2g | Protein 5g

GREEN SMOOTHIES/HOT SOUPS

Blazing Broccoli Smoothie

For persons weighing 77kg and over, increase the ingredients by one-third.

Preparation Time: 5 Mins

Cooking Time: 0 Mins

Servings: 3-4

Ingredients

- 1 cup spinach
- 1 cup broccoli
- 1 carrot, peeled
- 1 green pepper, cored
- ½ lime, peeled
- 2 cups purified water

Directions

1. Pour 1 cup of filtered water into a blender with the spinach, broccoli, carrots, and lime. After that, properly combine the ingredients.

2. Continue to mix in the remaining water until you achieve the desired consistency.

Nutrition

Calories: 325 | Carbs: 80g | Fat: 2g | Protein: 11g

Whey Berry Spinach Chia Smoothie

For persons weighing 77kg and over, increase the ingredients by one-third.

Preparation Time: 5 Mins

Cooking Time: 0 Mins

Servings: 1

Ingredients

- "½ cup berries (you can mix blueberries with blackberry or strawberries)"
- ½ cup almond milk
- ½ scoop whey protein
- ¼ cup spinach leaves
- ½ tbsp chia seeds

Directions

1. Wash all the fruits and vegetables thoroughly. Then, blend the fruits and veggies in a blender.

2. After pouring the liquid into a glass, take a whiff of it.

Nutrition

Calories: 275 | Carbs: 29g | Fat: 4g | Protein: 24g

Zucchini and Blueberry Smoothie

For persons weighing 77kg and over, increase the ingredients by one-third.

Preparation Time: 5 Mins

Cooking Time: 0 Mins

Servings: 2

Ingredients

- "1 cup of frozen blueberries"
- "1 cup unsweetened almond milk"
- "1 banana"
- "1 zucchini, skinned and sliced"

Directions

1. Put the ingredients into a blender with a high-powered motor and process until smooth.

2. Serve, and have fun with it!

Nutrition

Calories: 283 | Carbs: 40g | Fat: 10g | Protein: 13g

Tofu and Mushroom Soup

For persons weighing 77kg and over, increase the ingredients by one-third.

Preparation Time: 15 Mins

Cooking Time: 10 Mins

Servings: 4

Ingredients

- 2 tbsp olive oil"
- "1 garlic clove, crushed"
- "1 large yellow onion, finely sliced"
- "1 tsp freshly grated ginger"
- 1 cup vegetable stock
- "2 small potatoes, skinned and sliced"

- "¼ tsp salt"
- "¼ tsp black pepper"
- "2- 14 oz silken tofu, drained and washed"
- "2/3 cup baby Bella mushrooms, carved"
- "1 tbsp sliced fresh oregano"
- "2 tbsp sliced fresh parsley to garnish

Directions

1. Using a medium-sized pot on medium-moderate heat, gently sauté the garlic, onion, and ginger until the vegetables are soft and aromatic.

2. Include the vegetable stock and potatoes to a bowl and mix well. Cook for a further 12 minutes, or until the potatoes are fork-tender.

3. After stirring in the tofu, the ingredients should be pureed using an immersion blender until they are smooth.

4. Mix in the mushrooms and simmer with the pot covered until the mushrooms warm up while occasionally stirring to ensure that the tofu doesn't curdle, approximately 7 minutes.

5. Stir oregano and dish the soup. Garnish with parsley and serve immediately.

Nutrition

Calories 310 | Fat 10g | Protein 40.0g | Carbohydrates 0g

Chilled Avocado Soup

For persons weighing 77kg and over, increase the ingredients by one-third.

Preparation Time: 50 Mins

Cooking Time: 0 Mins

Servings: 2

Ingredients

- 3 medium ripe avocados, halved, seeded, peeled, and cut into chunks
- 2 cloves fresh garlic, crushed
- 2 cups low-sodium, fat-free chicken broth, divided
- ½ cucumber, skinned and sliced
- ½ cup sliced white onion
- ½ cup superbly chopped carrot
- Thin avocado slices for garnish
- Paprika to sprinkle
- Salt and recently crushed pepper to taste
- Hot red pepper sauce to taste

Directions

1. Remove six bowls from the freezer then allow them to come to room temperature for 30 minutes.

2. While you wait, put 1 cup of broth, garlic, cucumber, avocado, onion, and carrots in your blender. Make a smooth sauce by blending all of the ingredients together in a food processor or blender.

3. Include the leftover portion of the broth. If you want things spicy, sprinkle on some hot sauce and season with salt and pepper to taste. Re-blend the mixture until it is smooth, using all the components.

4. Pour the mixed ingredients into the cooled bowls. Refrigerate the bowls for a further hour this time.

5. Serve the soup with paprika and avocado slices on top when it's time to serve. To be served icy cold.

Nutrition

Calories: 255 | Protein: 4 g, Fat: 22 g, Carbs: 15 g

CHAPTER 9: PHASE 2

Shopping List

Fruits

Strawberries

Banana

Blueberries

Raspberries

Blackberries

Avocado

Pineapple

Apricots

Unsweetened cranberries

Green apples

Pear

Kiwis

Peaches

Dairy

Unsweetened almond milk

Peanut butter

Whey protein

Plain Greek yogurt, low-fat

Butter

Milk

Almond butter

Almond milk

Vegetables

Fresh tomatoes

Kale leaves

Spinach

Kale

Swiss chard

Basil

Broccoli florets

Carrot

Raw beets

Zucchini

Spinach leaves

Quinoa

Cauliflower florets

Bread

Whole-wheat English muffins

Baguette French bread or Italian bread

Celery

Oats

Wheat germ

Oils

Coconut oil

Olive oil

Vegetable oil'

Baking staples

All-purpose flour

Vanilla extract

Coconut flour

Baking powder

Baking soda

Eggs

Liquid egg whites

Dark pure maple syrup

Dry

Dark Chocolate

Dark chocolate chips

Vanilla protein powder

Plain protein powder

Chocolate protein powder

Protein supplement, powdered

White Sugar

Raw Almonds

Pumpkin seeds

Sunflower seeds

Walnut

Chia seeds

Dry dates

Cinnamon

Protein powder, vanilla-flavored hemp

Flax seeds

Shredded coconut (dry)

Erythritol sweetener (powdered)

Dark cocoa

Coconut flakes

Brown sugar

Stevia powder

Others

Cloves garlic

Lemon zest

Chamomile tea

Ice

Balsamic vinegar

Lime

Purified Water

Freshly grated ginger

Orange juice

Honey

Peanut butter

Pitted soft dates

Mini chocolate chips

Roasted pecan halves

Maple syrup

Applesauce

Nutmeg

Pumpkin puree, canned

Milk chocolate chips

Seasoning

Salt

Sea salt

Pepper

Chili powder

WHITE SMOOTHIE

Recovery Smoothie

For persons weighing 77kg and over, increase the ingredients by one-third.

Preparation Time: 5 Mins

Cooking Time: 0 Mins

Servings: 1

Ingredients

- ¼ banana (frozen)
- ½ cup orange juice
- ½ scoop whey protein
- ¼ cup pineapple

Directions

1. In a mixer, mix the ingredients.

2. After pouring the concoction into your glass, you can then enjoy it.

Nutrition

Calories: 320 | Carbs: 41g | Fat: 18g | Protein: 3g

Healthy Breakfast Sandwich

For persons weighing 77 kg and over, increase the ingredients by one-third.

Preparation Time: 5 mins

Cooking Time: 5 mins

Servings: 2

Ingredients

- 2 split whole-wheat English muffins
- ¾ cup of liquid egg whites
- 2 slices of fresh tomato
- ½ cup of spinach leaves

Directions

1. Use a nonstick skillet on a medium-low burner to cook the egg whites for around 4 minutes.

2. English muffins should be toasted.

3. Next, divide the egg whites that have been boiled between the bases of two muffins.

4. On top of each one, place a muffin cap, some spinach, and a tomato slice.

Nutrition

186 Calories | Protein 16.3g | Carbohydrates 28.8g | Fat 1.5g | Sodium 474mg

Blueberry Pancakes

For persons weighing 77 kg and over, increase the ingredients by one-third.

Preparation Time: 10 mins

Cooking Time: 10 mins

Servings: 2

Ingredients

- 1 ripe banana, cut into parts
- 1 tbsp chia seeds

- 2 eggs
- ½ tbsp dark cocoa powder (optional)
- 1 tbsp all-purpose flour
- ½ tbsp ground cinnamon (optional)
- 1 tweak of sea salt
- ½ tbsp vanilla extract (optional)
- ¼ cup of blueberries
- ½ tbsp coconut oil or more as required

Directions

1. A blender is all that is needed to incorporate the chia seeds.

2. Blend for around three to five sec until the mixture is finely powdered.

3. In a large mixing bowl or stand mixer with with the paddle attachment, combine the flour, sugar, cocoa powder, salt, cinnamon, and vanilla extract.

4. Heat a skillet to a medium-high temperature. Apply high-temperature to coconut oil in a large skillet over moderate heat.

5. Pour half of the batter into the oil. Add half of the blueberries onto the batter. Then cook it until the bubbles are formed, and the edges are dried for about 3 to 4 minutes.

6. Next, cook them while flipping until browned on both sides, for 2 to 3 minutes.

7. Repeat with the leftover blueberries and batter by using coconut oil if required.

Nutrition

233 Calories | Protein 8.2g | carbohydrates 22g | fat 13.5g | sodium 231.8mg

Breakfast Quinoa

For persons weighing 77 kg and over, increase the ingredients by one-third.

Preparation Time: 10 mins

Cooking Time: 15 mins

Servings: 4

Ingredients

- ¼ cup of chopped raw almonds
- 1 cup of quinoa
- 1 tbsp ground cinnamon
- 2 pitted, dried dates, chopped finely
- 2 cups of milk
- 1 tbsp vanilla extract
- 1 tbsp sea salt
- 2 tbsp honey
- 5 dried apricots, chopped finely

Directions

1. Once you've toasted the almonds for three to five mins, take them from the skillet and set them aside.

2. Cook the quinoa and cinnamon together until tender in a medium skillet over moderate heat. In a saucepan, combine milk and salt, and bring to a boil.

3. Reduce the heat to a simmer and cover the pan. Cook 15 minutes.

4. Mix the honey, quinoa, dates, almonds, and apricots in a large mixing basin. On top of each serving, scatter the remaining almonds.

Nutrition

327 Calories | Protein 11.5g | Carbohydrates 53.9g | Fat 7.9g | Sodium 501mg

High-Fiber Breakfast Bars

For persons weighing 77 kg and over, increase the ingredients by one-third.

Preparation Time: 15 mins

Cooking Time: 30 mins

Servings: 2

Ingredients

- 1-½ cups of oats
- Cooking spray
- ¼ cup of wheat germ
- 2 tbsp protein powder, vanilla-flavored hemp
- ¼ cup of ground flax seed
- 1 tbsp ground cinnamon
- 3 bananas
- ½ tbsp of salt
- ¼ cup of peanut butter, or according to taste
- 1 tbsp vanilla extract
- 2 tbsp honey

Directions

1. Adjust the temperature of the kiln to 375 degrees Fahrenheit.

2. Aluminum foil should be sprayed with cooking spray and then used to line a baking bowl measuring 8 by 8 inches.

3. The foil should reach over the sides of the pan.

4. A mixing dish should be used to combine the cereal. Using a separate dish, combine the mashed bananas, peanut butter, vanilla essence, and honey.

5. After combining the wet and dry ingredients, spread the mixture evenly in the prepared baking dish.

6. Cook for twenty mins in a preheated oven. On the top, spread one-quarter cup of peanut butter.

7. Continue baking for another 10 minutes till the center is well-done, and the sides are gently browned.

8. Lift the bars onto a cutting board with aluminum foil handles after they've finished cooling in the pan.

9. After cutting into bars, wrap them in plastic, and put them in the fridge.

Cook's Notes

- Any form of protein powder will suffice. Hemp is rich in fiber; therefore, you must use it.

- If you're using a sweet powder, consider cutting down on the honey. Also, slice the bars into individual portions when cooled and cover them in plastic wrap for a quick breakfast.

Nutrition

169 Calories | Protein 6.2g | Carbohydrates 21.3g | Fat 7.6g | Sodium 148mg

SNACKS

Lemon Fat Bombs

For persons weighing 77 kg and over, increase the ingredients by one-third.

Preparation Time: 10 minutes

Cooking Time: 50 minutes

Serving: 4

Ingredients

- 1 cup of shredded coconut (dry)
- ¼ cup of coconut oil
- 3 tbsp of erythritol sweetener (powdered)
- 1 tbsp of lemon zest
- 1 tweak of salt

Directions

1. Place the coconut in a powerful mixer and start it up.

2. Blend until creamy for 15 minutes. Add sweetener, coconut oil, salt, and lemon zest. Blend for 2 minutes.

3. Fill small muffin cups with the coconut mixture. Chill in the refrigerator for thirty minutes.

Nutrition

Calories: 156 | Carbs: 6g | Fat: 28g | Protein: 3g

Walnut Bites

For persons weighing 77 kg and over, increase the ingredients by one-third.

Preparation Time: 15 Mins

Cooking Time: 0 Mins

Serving: 16

Ingredients

- 1-½ cup old-fashioned oats
- 3 tbsp dark cocoa
- ½ tsp cinnamon
- 1 cup pitted soft dates
- 3 tbsp almond butter
- 3 tbsp dark untainted maple syrup
- 3 tbsp sliced walnuts
- 3 tbsp tiny chocolate chips

Directions

1. Crush the oatmeal and place it in a bowl for serving. Cocoa, cinnamon, and salt should be mixed together.

2. Crush dates, and add almond butter and maple syrup to make a thick paste.

3. During the next 2 minutes, shape the dough into the silicone to look like smashed cookie dough. Then, carrying on with the work on the dough, incorporate the chocolate chips and nuts into the mixture.

4. Knead well. Make a total of 14 balls. Refrigerate to adjust the chocolate.

Nutrition

Calories: 150 | Carbs: 16g | Fat: 8g | Protein: 2g

Tomato & Basil Bruschetta

For persons weighing 77 kg and over, increase the ingredients by one-third.

Preparation Time: 10 minutes

Cooking Time: 10 minutes

Servings: 3

Ingredients

- 3 tomatoes, chopped
- 1 piece of garlic, crushed
- ¼ tbsp garlic powder (optional)
- A few basil leaves, coarsely chopped
- Salt, as needed
- Pepper, as needed
- ½ tbsp olive oil
- ½ tbsp balsamic vinegar
- ½ tbsp of butter
- ½ baguette of French or Italian bread, sliced a half-inch-thick

Directions

1. Put the tomatoes, garlic, and basil in your bowl, and give everything a good toss. Drizzle oil plus vinegar, toss well, and set aside within an hour.

2. Dissolve the butter, then brush it over your baguette slices—place in your oven and toast.

3. After topping with the tomato mixture, it should be served immediately.

Nutrition

Calories 152 | Fat 4g | Carbs 29g | Protein 4g

Cauliflower Poppers

For persons weighing 77 kg and over, increase the ingredients by one-third.

Preparation Time: 20 minutes

Cooking Time: 30 minutes

Servings: 4

Ingredients

- 4 cups cauliflower florets
- 2 tsp olive oil
- ¼ tsp chili powder
- Pepper and salt, as needed

Directions

1. Preheat the oven to 450°F. Prepare a roasting pan by greasing it.

2. Put the ingredients into the bowl and give it a good toss to coat everything.

3. The cauliflower mixture should be transferred into a roasting pan that has been prepared and spread out in a uniform layer. Cook for around 25 to 30 minutes at 400°F. To be served hot.

Nutrition

Calories: 152 | Fat: 8.5 g | Carbs: 2.1 g | Protein: 4.2 g

Trail Mix

For persons weighing 77 kg and over, increase the ingredients by one-third.

Preparation Time: 5 minutes

Cooking Time: 0 minutes

Servings: 3

Ingredients

- ½ cup salted pumpkin seeds

- ½ cup slivered almonds
- ¾ cup roasted pecan halves
- ¾ cup unsweetened cranberries
- 1 cup toasted coconut flakes

Directions

1. Place the almonds and pecans in a pan over medium heat. Heat for two to three minutes, then set aside to cool. After the mixture has been allowed to cool, place all of the components inside of a sizable plastic bag that has the ability to be sealed.

2. In the sealed bag, give it a good shake to combine everything. Then, evenly divide into suggested servings and store in airtight meal prep containers.

Nutrition

Calories: 158 | Fat: 1.2 g | Carbs: 1.1 g | Protein: 3.2 g

RED SMOOTHIES

Triple Berry Smoothie

For persons weighing 77 kg and over, increase the ingredients by one-third.

Preparation Time: 5 Mins

Cooking Time: 0 Mins

Servings: 2

Ingredients

- 1 cup crushed ice, divided
- ½ cup unsweetened almond milk
- 1 tbsp coconut oil
- ½ cup blueberries
- ½ cup raspberries
- ½ cup blackberries
- ½ tsp pure vanilla extract

Directions

1. Mix the almond milk, half cup of ice, and coconut oil in a mixer.

2. Mix in every type of berry, the vanilla extract, and the remaining half cup of ice.

3. After blending to a smooth consistency, serve.

Nutrition

Calories: 290 | Fat: 22g | Protein: 3g | Carbs: 10g

Spinach and Green Apple Smoothie

For persons weighing 77 kg and over, increase the ingredients by one-third.

Preparation Time: 5 Mins

Cooking Time: 0 Mins

Servings: 2

Ingredients

- 3 to 4 ice cubes
- 1 cup unsweetened almond milk
- 1 banana, peeled and chopped
- 2 green apples, peeled and chopped
- 1 cup raw spinach leaves
- 3 to 4 dates, pitted

- 1 tbsp grated ginger

Directions

1. Place the components in a mixer with a high-powered motor and process until smooth.

2. Serve, and have fun with it!

Nutrition

Calories: 290 | Carbs: 47g | Fat: 1g | Protein: 24g

Apricot, Strawberry, and Banana Smoothie

For persons weighing 77kg and over, increase the ingredients by one-third.

Preparation Time: 5 Mins

Cooking Time: 0 Mins

Servings: 2

Ingredients

1. 1 frozen banana
2. 11 x 2 cups almond milk
3. 5 dried apricots
4. 1 cup fresh strawberries

Directions

1. Place the components into a blender with a high-powered motor and process until smooth.

2. Serve, and have fun with it!

Nutrition

Calories: 148 | Carbs: 28g | Fat: 0g | Protein: 2g

Papaya Smoothie

For persons weighing 77 kg and over, increase the ingredients by one-third.

Preparation Time: 5 Mins

Cooking Time: 0 Mins

Servings: 2

Ingredients

- 2 to 3 frozen broccoli florets
- 1 cup orange juice
- 1 small ripe avocado, skinned, cored, and chopped
- 1 cup papaya
- 1 cup of fresh strawberries

Directions

1. Place the components into a blender with a high-powered motor, and process until smooth.

2. Serve, and have fun with it!

Nutrition

Calories: 316 | Carbs: 79g | Fat: 1g | Protein: 3g

Kale and Kiwi Smoothie

For persons weighing 77 kg and over, increase the ingredients by one-third.

Preparation Time: 5 Mins

Cooking Time: 0 Mins

Servings: 2

Ingredients

- 2 to 3 ice cubes
- 1 cup orange juice
- 1 small pear, skinned and sliced
- 2 kiwis, skinned and sliced
- 2 to 3 kale leaves
- 2 to 3 dates, pitted

Directions

1. Put the components into a blender with a high-powered motor, and process until smooth.

2. Serve, and have fun with it!

Nutrition

Calories: 277 | Carbs: 68g | Fat: 0g | Protein: 1g

SNACKS 2

Protein Bars

For persons weighing 77 kg and over, increase the ingredients by one-third.

Preparation Time: 15 Mins

Cooking Time: 15 Mins

Servings: 2

Ingredients

- ½ sunflower seeds
- 3 cups of rolled oats
- ½ shredded coconut, unsweetened
- 1 tbsp ground cinnamon
- ¼ cup brown sugar
- 1 tbsp sea salt
- ½ cup melted peanut butter
- 1 cup yogurt, plain Greek
- 6 tbsp pure maple syrup
- 1 tbsp vanilla extract
- ¼ cup melted coconut oil
- 1- 2 oz chopped bar of dark chocolate
- 1cup vanilla protein powder

Directions

1. Turn the oven on to 350⁰F and let it preheat.

2. Grease a baking dish that is 13 inches wide and 9 inches deep.

3. Combine in a large bowl the following ingredients: oats, coconut, sunflower seeds, cinnamon, sea salt, and brown sugar.

4. Pour all of the ingredients into their individual bowls and mix them together until they are very smooth.

5. Mix thoroughly after including in the oats.

6. After combining the chocolate and protein powder in a basin for mixing, pour the mixture onto a prepared baking dish.

7. Bake in a hot oven for 15 minutes, until the food is golden brown.

Nutrition

330 Calories | Protein 23.8g | Carbohydrates 25.5g | Fat 16g | Sodium 243.7mg

Zucchini Protein Pancakes

For persons weighing 77 kg and over, increase the ingredients by one-third.

Preparation Time: 10 Mins

Cooking Time: 5 Mins

Servings: 2

Ingredients

- 1 small shredded zucchini
- ½ cup oats, old-fashioned
- 1 egg
- 1 scoop of protein powder
- 2 tbsp coconut flour
- Cooking spray
- 1 tbsp Stevia powder

Directions

1. Put the oats in a blender and grind until they become a granular consistency (3 to 4 poundings).

2. To make a batter, combine the oats, egg, zucchini, coconut flour, stevia, and protein powder in a blending container and mix till it is smooth.

3. While heating up, sprinkle some cooking spray on them to oil the pan.

4. Next, the batter should be poured into the pan.

5. After around 3 minutes of cooking, the edges should look dry.

6. Cook for an additional two minutes while turning the meat.

Nutrition

Calories 364 | Protein 28.8g | Carbohydrates 48.3g | Fat 9.1g | Sodium 267.1mg

Chocolate Protein Muffins

For persons weighing 77 kg and over, increase the ingredients by one-third.

Preparation Time: 10 mins

Cooking Time: 20 mins

Servings: 2

Ingredients

- ¾ cup flour, all-purpose
- 2 packets of chocolate protein powder
- ½ tbsp baking soda
- ¼ tbsp salt
- ½ tbsp baking powder
- ½ cup applesauce
- ⅓ cup of white sugar
- ½ cup plain Greek yogurt, low-fat
- 1 egg
- ½ cup of dark chocolate chips
- ¾ tbsp vanilla extract

Directions

1. Pre-heat your oven to a temperature of up to 400°F.

2. Add flour, baking soda, salt, and baking powder to a large basin, and whisk them together until they resemble fine crumbs.

3. Stir together the yoghurt, applesauce and sugar in a large bowl until well-combined. Mix well. Additionally, add the flour mixture. After giving it a good swirl, wrinkle in the chocolate chips.

4. Create the muffins and place them in a baking try using nonstick spray or cupcake linings.

5. Bake for seven minutes in the oven at 400°F, after which you should lower the temperature to 350°F.

6. Bake until the muffins spring back (when touched) for 10 to 12 minutes.

Nutrition

170 Calories 170 | Protein 4.1g | Carbohydrates 29.9g | Fat 4.4g | Sodium 199.6mg

Protein Pumpkin Muffins

For persons weighing 77 kg and over, increase the ingredients by one-third.

Preparation Time: 5 Mins

Cooking Time: 17 Mins

Servings: 2

Ingredients

- 1-½ cups flour, all-purpose
- 2 cups protein supplement, powdered
- 1-½ tbsp salt
- 2 tbsp ground cinnamon
- 2 tbsp ground nutmeg
- 1 cup white sugar
- 1-½ cups applesauce
- 1 cup vegetable oil
- 2 eggs
- 1- 15 oz can of pumpkin puree
- 2 egg whites
- 1 cup walnuts, chopped
- ½ cup of water

Directions

1. Up to 350°F, preheat your oven. Grease the muffin cups using muffin liners.

2. In a bowl, mix the components for the protein powder cookie dough: flour, salt, cinnamon, sugar, and nutmeg. After adding the applesauce, oil, eggs, pumpkin, water, and egg whites, ensure everything is thoroughly combined.

3. Fold in walnuts, then spoon batter into the muffin cups.

4. If you poke a toothpick halfway through the centre of one of the muffins, it should come out clean, which takes 16 minutes at 375°F.

Nutrition

Calories 246 | Protein 10g | Carbohydrates 22.2g | Fat 13.4g | Sodium 285.5mg

Chocolate Chip Oatmeal Protein Cookies

For persons weighing 77 kg and over, increase the ingredients by one-third.

Preparation Time: 15 Mins

Cooking Time: 10 Mins

Servings: 2

Ingredients

- ½ cup of milk chocolate chips
- 2 cups of quick-cooking oats
- ½ cup white sugar
- 1 tbsp baking soda
- 2 scoops of vanilla protein powder
- ¼ tbsp of salt
- 2 large eggs
- 6 tbsp smooth peanut butter
- 1 tbsp vanilla extract

Directions

1. Turn the oven up to 350°F.

2. In an average-sized blending bowl, mix the protein powder, salt, baking soda, sugar, and chocolate chips with the chocolate chips.

3. In a bowl, mix peanut butter, one egg, and vanilla extract with the vanilla extract.

4. Include the remaining egg in the mixture.

5. Knead the dough until it becomes sticky and thick.

6. Put tablespoons of dough, two inches aside, on parchment paper-lined baking sheets. Bake for 30 minutes. To flatten the cookies, use your palm to gently press on them.

7. Bake for 10 minutes in an oven that has been prepared until the bottoms and edges are a golden-brown color.

8. Remove it to a cooling rack and allow to cool for an additional 2 minutes after removing from pan.

Nutrition

Calories 110 | Protein 6g | Carbohydrates 12.5g | Fat 4.4g | Sodium 130.6mg

GREEN SMOOTHIES/HOT SOUPS

Mean Green Smoothie

For persons weighing 77 kg and over, increase the ingredients by one-third.

Preparation Time: 5 Mins

Cooking Time: 0 Mins

Servings: 2

Ingredients

- 1-½ cups crushed ice, divided
- 1 cup kale, tightly packed, cleaned
- ½ cup spinach, cleaned
- ½ cup Swiss chard, cleaned
- 2 tbsp coconut oil
- 2 tbsp chia seeds
- ½ cup of water

Directions

1. Blend a three-quarter cup of ice mixed with Swiss chard, kale, and spinach leaves in a mixer.

2. Mix in the remaining three-quarter cup of ice, the coconut oil, and the chia seeds.

3. After blending for one minute, or until smooth, serve the mixture immediately.

Nutrition

Calories: 293 | Fat: 23g | Protein: 8g | Carbs: 3g

Avocado Spinach Smoothie

For persons weighing 77 kg and over, increase the ingredients by one-third.

Preparation Time: 5 Mins

Cooking Time: 0 Mins

Servings: 2

Ingredients

- 1 cup spinach
- 2 avocados, peeled and seeds removed
- 1 lime, peeled
- 1 cup purified water

Directions

1. Put the spinach, avocados, and lime into a blender and a half cup of water and process the blend until it is completely even.

2. Blend in the remaining water until the desired texture is attained.

Nutrition

Calories: 288 | Fat: 15g | Protein: 8g | Carbs: 13g

Chamomile, Peach, and Ginger Smoothie

For persons weighing 77 kg and over, increase the ingredients by one-third.

Preparation Time: 5 Mins

Cooking Time: 0 Mins

Servings: 2

Ingredients

- 4 to 5 ice cubes
- 1 cup chamomile tea
- 1 lime, juiced
- 2 large peaches, chopped
- 1tbsp grated ginger

Directions

1. Put the components into a mixer with a high-powered motor and process until smooth.

2. Serve, and have fun with it!

Nutrition

Calories: 275 | Carbs: 48g | Fat: 1g | Protein: 3g

Peach and Cucumber Smoothie

For persons weighing 77 kg and over, increase the ingredients by one-third.

Preparation Time: 5 Mins

Cooking Time: 0 Mins

Servings: 2

Ingredients

- 2 to 3 ice cubes
- 1 small cucumber, skinned and sliced
- ½ banana, peeled and chopped
- 1 large peach, chopped

Directions

1. Combine the ice, water, banana, peach, and cucumber in a high-speed blender.

2. Blend until smooth and serve.

Nutrition

Calories: 260 | Carbs: 67g | Fat: 0g | Protein: 1g

Detox Support Smoothie

For persons weighing 77 kg and over, increase the ingredients by one-third.

Preparation Time: 5 Mins

Cooking Time: 0 Mins

Servings: 2

Ingredients

- 1 to 2 ice cubes
- 1 cup water
- ½ avocado, sliced
- 2 carrots, sliced
- ½ raw beet, peeled and chopped
- ½ lemon, juiced

Directions

1. Put the components in a mixer with a high-powered motor and process till completely even.

2. Place the liquid in the glasses, serve and have fun with it!

Nutrition

Calories: 370 | Carbs: 49g | Fat: 18g | Protein: 9g

CHAPTER 10: Phase 3

Shopping list

Fruits

Oranges

Fresh cranberries

Banana

Blueberries

Mango

Red grapes

Avocado

Pineapple

Frozen spinach cubes

Pear

Papaya

Apple

Dried cranberries

Dairy

Vegan butter

Coconut milk

Coconut Cream

Butter

Cocoa whey protein powder

Whey protein powder

Greek yogurt, plain

Eggs

Skim milk

Mayonnaise

Almond butter

Vegetables

Jalapeño

Cilantro

Red cabbage

Kale

Parsley

Cabbage

Canned chickpeas

Scallions

Lettuce leaves

Dip

Celery

Cauliflower

Canned artichoke hearts

Cherry tomatoes

Iceberg lettuce

Spinach

Cucumber

Carrot

Zucchini

Yellow onion

Cereals

rolled oats, old-fashioned

Wheat cereal

Oats

Meat

Ground turkey

Ground pork

Chicken breast

Oils

Olive oil

Grapeseed oil

Sesame oil

Baking staples

Almond flour

Vanilla extract

Granulated sweetener

Vanilla

Baking powder

Baking Soda

Whole wheat flour

Dry

Bok choy leaves

Thai or sweet basil leaves

Onion powder

Garlic powder

Ground cinnamon

Green tea

Sugar

Pumpkin seeds

Coffee

Walnut

Ground flax seeds

Chia seeds

Others

Agave nectar

Sour cream

Halved sugar snap peas

Chicken stock

Soy sauce

Stevia-erythritol sweetener

Peanut butter-flavored syrup

Honey peanut butter

Ricotta cheese, whole milk

Maple syrup

Canned heart of palm

Agave syrup

Cooked spelled noodles

Chives

Rice vinegar

Sambal

pickle rounds

Homemade hummus

Spelled flour tortillas

Garbanzo beans

Canned chickpeas

Canned pumpkin

Maple sugar

Pumpkin pie spice

Whipped cream cheese

Canned mandarin oranges

Orange juice

Pitted dates

Cloves garlic

Ice

Lime juice

freshly grated ginger

Chocolate chips

Applesauce

Honey

Jelly

Vegetable broth

Mint leaves

Seasoning

Ground black pepper

Cayenne pepper

Curry powder

Ground white pepper

Cumin powder

Nutmeg powder

Salt

Pepper

Sea salt

WHITE SMOOTHIES

Tropical Fast Smoothie

For persons weighing 77 kg and over, increase the ingredients by one-third.

Preparation Time: 5 Mins

Cooking Time: 0 Mins

Servings: 2

Ingredients

- ½ cup kale
- ½ cup spinach
- 2 cups coconut milk
- ½ cup frozen mango
- ½ cup frozen pineapple

Directions

1. Use a blender to combine the fresh fruits and vegetables.

2. Pour mixture into your glass and serve.

Nutrition

Calories: 280 | Carbs: 68g | Fat: 0g | Protein: 0g

Superfood Blueberry Smoothie

For persons weighing 77 kg and over, increase the ingredients by one-third.

Preparation Time: 5 minutes

Cooking Time: 0 minutes

Servings: 2

Ingredients

- 2 to 3 cubes frozen spinach
- 1 cup green tea
- 1 banana
- 2 cups blueberries
- 1 tbsp ground flaxseed

Directions

1. Place the ingredients into a mixer with a high-powered motor and process till even.

2. Serve, and have fun with it!

Nutrition:

Calories: 283 | Carbs: 52g | Fat: 0g | Protein: 2g

Pear and Spinach Smoothie

For persons weighing 77 kg and over, increase the ingredients by one-third.

Preparation Time: 5 minutes

Cooking Time: 0 minutes

Servings: 2

Ingredients

- 2 to 3 ice-covered spinach cubes
- 1 cup orange juice
- 2 large pears, peeled and chopped
- 1 tbsp ground flaxseed

Directions

1. Place the ingredients into a mixer with a high-powered motor and process till even.

2. Serve, and have fun with it!

Nutrition

Calories: 270 | Carbs: 59g | Fat: 0g | Protein: 4g

Mango and Cucumber Smoothie

For persons weighing 77 kg and over, increase the ingredients by one-third.

Preparation Time: 5 Mins

Cooking Time: 0 Mins

Servings: 2

Ingredients

- ½ cup crushed ice or 3 to 4 ice cubes
- 1 cup coconut milk
- 1 mango, skinned and chopped
- 1 small cucumber, skinned and sliced
- 1 to 2 dates, pitted
- 1 tbsp chia seeds

Directions

1. Put the fixings into a mixer with a high-powered motor and process until it becomes even.

2. Serve, and have fun with it!

Nutrition

Calories: 320 | Carbs: 44g | Fat: 2g | Protein: 30g

High-Fiber Fruit Smoothie

For persons weighing 77 kg and over, increase the ingredients by one-third.

Preparation Time: 5 Mins

Cooking Time: 0 Mins

Servings: 2

Ingredients

- 1 frozen banana, chopped
- 1 cup orange juice
- 2 cups chopped papaya
- 1 cup shredded cabbage
- 1 tbsp chia seeds

Directions

3. Put the fixings into a mixer with a high-powered motor and process till it becomes even.

4. Serve, and have fun with it!

Nutrition

Calories: 278 | Carbs: 26g | Fat: 4g | Protein: 7g

SNACKS

Protein-Rich Granola Bars

For persons weighing 77 kg and over, increase the ingredients by one-third.

Preparation Time: 20 Mins

Cooking Time: 12 Mins

Servings: 2

Ingredients

- 1 cup canned chickpeas, drained

- Cooking spray
- 2 egg whites
- 1-½ cups rolled oats, old-fashioned
- 1 small and grated apple
- 1 cup wheat cereal, puffed
- ½ cup chocolate chips, mini semisweet
- ½ cup applesauce
- ¼ cup honey
- ¼ cup dried cranberries, sweetened
- ¼ cup of almond butter
- ½ tsp ground cinnamon
- ¼ cup chopped almonds

Directions

1. Turn the oven on to 350⁰F and let it preheat.

2. Using cooking spray, grease a small muffin tray.

3. Egg whites and chickpeas should be mixed together in a food processor until they are completely integrated.

4. The chickpea mixture should come up about halfway in a bowl. Mix together the oats, apple, puffed wheat, chocolate chips, applesauce, honey, cranberries, almond butter, and almonds until everything is evenly distributed throughout the mixture.

5. Put the batter into the muffin tins that have been prepared and smooth it up with a fork.

6. Bake in an oven that has been prepared for about 12 mins, or until the edges are browned.

Nutrition

Calories 192 | Protein 4.9g | Carbohydrates 28.8g | Fat 7.7g | Sodium 94.5mg

Protein Crepes

For persons weighing 77 kg and over, increase the ingredients by one-third.

Preparation Time: 10 Mins

Cooking Time: 10 Mins

Servings: 2

Ingredients

- 1 cup skim milk
- 1 cup of whole wheat flour
- 1 pinch of ground cinnamon, or according to taste
- 4 egg whites
- 1 tbsp ground cinnamon
- 1 tbsp olive oil
- Olive oil cooking spray
- 1 tbsp jelly
- 1 cup Greek yogurt, plain fat-free

Directions

1. To make a smooth batter, whisk egg whites, milk, flour, olive oil, and cinnamon together in a large mixing dish.

2. Place a skillet on the stove over moderate heat and coat it lightly with cooking spray. Before adding the batter, make sure the skillet is well-coated with a thin layer of batter by pouring in a quarter cup and rotating it slowly. Cook for about two minutes, or until the underside is beginning to become a very pale golden brown. Cook for an additional two minutes on the other side, or until the bottom

is just beginning to become golden in colour. Then, continue with the remaining batter.

3. Jelly and Greek yogurt should be combined and mixed together in a bowl. Fill every crepe with a layer of yogurt combination and wrap it around the filling. Serve the remaining yogurt mixture on the plates' rolled crepes. Cinnamon should be sprinkled on each crepe.

Nutrition

Calories 430 | Protein 29.6g | Carbohydrates 62.8g | Fat 8.1g | Sodium 210.4mg

High-Protein Torte

For persons weighing 77 kg and over, increase the ingredients by one-third.

Preparation Time: 20 Mins

Cooking Time: 30 Mins

Servings: 8

Ingredients

• Garbanzo beans, rinsed

• 1- 19 oz can chickpeas

• 4 eggs

• 1 cup Splenda or sugar

• 1- 15 oz can pumpkin

• 2 tbsp maple sugar

• 2 tbsp pumpkin pie spice

• ¼ cup of walnut halves

• 6 tbsp baking powder

• 6 oz whipped cream cheese

• 1- 11 oz drained, can mandarin oranges

• 2 cups sugar, powdered

Directions

1. Turn the oven to 350°F. Blend or pulse the eggs and chickpeas together in a food processor until the mixture is smooth. Blend until smooth while adding the Splenda, pumpkin, syrup, spice, and baking powder.

2. Spray a circular cake pan measuring 8 inches in diameter with cooking spray. The batter should reach about halfway up the cup. Bake for approximately 1 hour, or until a knife inserted in the center comes out clean. Because the cake is so delicate, you need to wait until it has completely cooled before attempting to remove it from the pan.

3. Compose the granulated sugar and cream cheese in a bowl and stir until smooth and combined well. After that, use the icing to decorate the cake's edges and top. Decorated with walnuts and mandarin oranges, this dish has a distinct flavour.

Nutrition

Calories 368 | Protein 8.9g | Carbohydrates 59.4g | Fat 12g | Sodium 489.6mg

Hummus Zucchini Wrap

For persons weighing 77 kg and over, increase the ingredients by one-third.

Preparation Time: 10 Mins

Cooking Time: 8 Mins

Servings: 2

Ingredients

• ½ cup iceberg lettuce

• 1 zucchini, sliced

• 2 cherry tomatoes, sliced

- 2 spelled flour tortillas
- 4 tbsp homemade hummus
- ¼ tsp salt
- ⅛ tsp cayenne pepper
- 1 tbsp grapeseed oil

Directions

1. Take a grill pan, coat it with oil, and put it on a heat setting between medium and high.

2. In the meantime, prepare a big plate for the zucchini slices by laying them out in a single layer. After you have seasoned them with salt and cayenne pepper, spritz some oil on them and toss them until they are completely covered in oil.

3. Place the zucchini slices on the grill pan in a single layer and cook for two to three mins on every side, until either grill markings emerge.

4. Assemble tortillas, and for this, heat the tortilla on the grill pan until warm, develop grill marks, and spread two tablespoons of hummus over each tortilla.

5. Distribute grilled zucchini slices over the tortillas, top with lettuce and tomato slices, and wrap tightly.

Nutrition

Calories 264.5 | Fats 5.1g | Protein 8.5g | Carbs 34.5g

Turkey Burger Bites

For persons weighing 77 kg and over, increase the ingredients by one-third.

Preparation time: 15 Mins

Cooking time: 0 Mins

Servings: 24 bites

Ingredients:

- 1 lb ground turkey
- ½ tsp of salt
- ¼ tsp onion powder
- ⅛ teaspoon freshly ground black pepper
- ½ tsp garlic powder
- 24 pickle rounds
- 12 cherry tomatoes, halved

Directions

1. Raise the temperature in the oven to 405 degrees Fahrenheit. It is important to line a baking sheet with parchment paper before beginning.

2. Mix the ground turkey, salt, onion powder, black pepper, and garlic powder in a medium bowl.

3. Spoon a teaspoon of mixture onto the prepared baking sheet and shape into mini burger patties. Bake for 15 minutes, or until a temperature of 165°F is attained on the inside.

4. Take the item out of the oven and let it cool.

5. Once cooled, slide each mini patty onto a toothpick. Add 1 pickle round and 1 tomato half to each toothpick. Serve, and have fun with it!

Nutrition

Calories: 155 | Fat: 6g | Protein: 15g | Carbs: 8g

LUNCH

Chilled Avocado and Cucumber Soup with Basil

For persons weighing 77 kg and over, increase the ingredients by one-third.

Preparation time: 15 minutes + chilling time

Cooking time: 0 minutes

Servings: 2

Ingredients

- 2 ripe avocados, pitted and peeled
- 2 large cucumbers, peeled and seeded
- 1- 13.5 oz can full-fat coconut milk
- 1 tbsp lime juice
- 2 tsp rice vinegar
- 1 tsp sambal
- Kosher salt, as needed
- 1 tbsp olive oil
- ½ cup fresh Thai or sweet basil leaves
- 1 tbsp chopped fresh chives

Directions

1. Put the flesh of the avocado and cucumber into a blender together with the flesh of the cucumber, lime juice, rice vinegar, sambal, and salt to taste, and purée the mixture until it is smooth.

2. It is possible that the mixture will require additional water to be added to it on a tablespoon-by-tablespoon basis in order to attain the consistency of pancake batter.

3. Place the soup in the refrigerator for at least 30 minutes and up to 3 hours.

4. Sprinkle some basil and chives on each plate and pour olive oil over it for presentation. To be served chilled.

Nutrition

Calories: 426 | Fat: 40g | Carbs: 20g | Protein: 5g

Basil and Avocado Salad

For persons weighing 77 kg and over, increase the ingredients by one-third.

Preparation Time: 10 Mins

Cooking Time: 0 Mins

Servings: 2

Ingredients

- ½ cup avocado, peeled, pitted, sliced
- ½ cup basil leaves
- ½ cup cherry tomatoes
- 2 cups cooked spelled noodles
- 1 tsp agave syrup
- 1 tbsp key lime juice
- 2 tbsp olive oil

Directions

1. Place the pasta in a large bowl, then include the tomato, avocado, and basil, and

give the mixture a thorough stir to integrate the ingredients.

2. Place some agave syrup and salt in a shallow container, followed by the addition of lime juice and olive oil, and then combine all of the ingredients until they are well integrated.

3. After adding the lime juice combination to the pasta, toss it together until everything is evenly distributed, and then serve.

Nutrition

Calories 387 | Fats 16.6 g | Protein 9.4g | Carbs 54.3g

Spinach and Kale Soup

For persons weighing 77 kg and over, increase the ingredients by one-third.

Preparation Time: 5 Mins

Cooking Time: 5 Mins

Servings: 2

Ingredients

- 3 oz vegan butter
- 1 cup fresh spinach, sliced coarsely
- 1 cup fresh kale, sliced coarsely
- 1 large avocado
- 3 tbsp sliced fresh mint leaves
- 3-½ cups coconut cream
- 1 cup vegetable broth
- Salt and black pepper to taste
- 1 lime, juiced

Directions

1. The vegan butter should be melted in a pot of about medium size over medium heat. The kale and spinach should be sautéed for about three mins, or till they have been wilted. Take the saucepan off the heat immediately.

2. When you have finished mixing in the other components, use an immersion blender to purée the soup until it has reached the desired velvety smoothness. While the soup is still hot, serve it to the guests.

Nutrition

Calories 380 | Fat 10 g | Protein 20 g | Carbs 30 g

Parsley, Spinach, and Walnut Pesto Salad

For persons weighing 77 kg and over, increase the ingredients by one-third.

Preparation time: 15 Mins

Cooking time: 0 Mins

Servings: 2

Ingredients

- 4 loosely packed cups baby spinach
- 2 loosely packed cups fresh flat-leaf parsley leaves
- 2 garlic cloves, peeled
- 1 cup walnut, toasted
- Grated zest and juice of one lemon
- ¼ cup olive oil
- ½ tsp kosher salt
- ½ tsp cracked black pepper
- 1-pint cherry tomatoes, halved
- 1-14 oz can artichoke hearts, quartered
- 1- 14 oz can hearts of palm, drained and cut into bite-sized pieces

Directions

1. Spinach, parsley, garlic, walnuts, lemon zest and juice, olive oil, salt, and black pepper should be combined in a food processor. The mixture should then be seasoned with salt and black pepper.

2. Pulse until everything is incorporated into a bright green pesto.

3. A large bowl should be used for the pesto. Immediately after you add the tomatoes, artichokes, and hearts of palm onto a dish, you should mix them all together with the dressing. Enjoy yourself while you're doing it!. Serve, and have fun with it!

Nutrition

Calories: 419 | Fat: 34g | Carbs: 24g | Protein: 14g

Warm Red Cabbage Salad with Walnuts

For persons weighing 77 kg and over, increase the ingredients by one-third.

Preparation time: 20 Mins

Cooking time: 10 Mins

Servings: 2

Ingredients

- 1 medium head red cabbage, thinly sliced
- 14 oz cup chopped toasted walnuts
- 2 teaspoons minced garlic
- ¼ cup balsamic vinegar
- 1 tbsp chopped fresh thyme
- 2 tbsp olive oil
- 14 oz tsp kosher salt
- ¼ tsp freshly ground black pepper

Directions

1. Combine chopped walnuts, garlic, and vinegar in a large bowl and mix well. Toss the ingredients together until the cabbage is well covered in the sauce.

2. Heat a big skillet to high heat.

3. When the pan is hot, add the olive oil and then the cabbage mixture.

4. Shake the pan to keep the cabbage moving as you cook it for 5 to 7 minutes, until warmed through but still a bit crisp.

5. Serve immediately with a generous sprinkling of salt and black pepper.

Nutrition

Calories: 277 | Fat: 22g | Carbs: 16g | Protein: 8g

SNACKS 2

Almond Paleo Date Cookies

For persons weighing 77 kg and over, increase the ingredients by one-third.

Preparation Time: 25 Mins

Cooking Time: 15 Mins

Servings: 24

Ingredients

- 1 cup of dates, sliced and pitted

- 1 tbsp vanilla extract
- 2-½ cups of almond flour, blanched
- ½ cup cherries, chopped and dried
- 2 tbsp chia seeds
- ½ cup walnuts, chopped
- ½ cup of coconut oil
- ½ tsp of sea salt
- ½ tsp baking soda
- 1 egg
- 2 tbsp of maple syrup

Directions

1. Turn raise the oven temperature to 400 degrees Fahrenheit. Then, line two baking pans with parchment paper.

2. To make the bars, whisk together the almond flour, dates, cherries, chia seeds, walnuts, and baking soda in a large mixing bowl. A dough should form once the egg, coconut oil, vanilla extract, and maple syrup have been well mixed together using a fork or spoon.

3. Using a tiny cookie scoop, spoon dough onto baking sheets.

4. Bake in an already heated oven for 15 minutes, or until the edges begin to brown. After turning off the oven, let the cookies inside for 10 more minutes with the door shut. Then, take the food out of the oven and let it cool down.

Nutrition

Calories 174 | Protein 3.8g | Carbohydrates 12.3g | Fat 13g | Sodium 66.7mg

Protein Truffles

For persons weighing 77 kg and over, increase the ingredients by one-third.

Preparation Time: 10 Mins

Cooking Time: 0 Mins

Servings: 20

Ingredients

- ½ cup honey peanut butter, roasted
- ½ cup ricotta cheese, whole milk
- ⅓ cup dry roasted peanuts, chopped
- 2 tbsp peanut butter-flavored syrup, sugar-free
- 2 scoops of vanilla protein powder
- 1 tsp vanilla extract
- 1 pinch of salt
- 2 packets of Stevia-erythritol sweetener

Directions

1. Ricotta cheese and peanut butter syrup should be combined with the other ingredients in a bowl. An electric hand mixer works great for this. Then, add salt and protein powder to taste and puree until well-combined.

2. Roll the mixture into 1-inch balls. Coat in diced peanuts.

3. Refrigerate till ready to serve.

Nutrition

70 Calories | Protein 5.9g | Carbohydrates 2.3g | Fat 4.6g | Sodium 78.1mg

Protein-Rich Peanut Butter Balls

For persons weighing 77 kg and over, increase the ingredients by one-third.

Preparation Time: 20 mins

Cooking Time: 2 hours

Servings: 2

Ingredients

- 2 scoops of protein powder, cocoa whey
- 2 cups peanut butter, crunchy
- 2 tbsp flax seeds
- 2 ripe and mashed bananas

Directions

1. Combine cocoa whey powder, peanut butter, flaxseed, and bananas in a big bowl.

2. In a walnut-size ball, squeeze in the mixture and put them in a tray covered with parchment (to separate the layers).

3. Thaw for about 2 hours before serving after being frozen.

Nutrition

136 Calories | Protein 5.3g | Carbohydrates 7g | Fat 10.8g | Sodium 101.6mg

---

Spinach Pie

For persons weighing 77 kg and over, increase the ingredients by one-third.

Preparation time: 15 Mins

Cooking time: 30 Mins

Servings: 2

Ingredients

- Olive oil
- 1 medium yellow onion, peeled and chopped
- 1-16 oz package frozen spinach, chopped, thawed & drained
- ¼ cup chopped scallions
- ⅛ tsp ground nutmeg
- 1 tsp garlic salt
- 6 large eggs, beaten

Directions

1. Preheat the oven to 350°F. Grease a pie plate that is 9 inches in diameter.

2. Add olive oil to a medium-sized pan and bring to a boil. Continue to sauté the onion for approximately four mins after it has been added, or until it has softened. Continue to boil the spinach for an additional three minutes after adding it to the pot.

3. Stir the additional components in a medium-sized bowl. Add the spinach mixture and whisk until everything is thoroughly combined.

4. Pour the prepared mixture into a pie pan and bake for 30 mins, until either the eggs have set. Remove from the oven and cool slightly before serving.

Nutrition

Calories: 399 | Fat: 30g | Protein: 25g | Carbs: 7g

Coffee Walnut Bars

For persons weighing 77 kg and over, increase the ingredients by one-third.

Preparation time: 15 Mins

Cooking time: 15 Mins

Servings: 14 bars

Ingredients

- 110g butter, melted
- 125ml coffee
- 60g coconut flour

- 55g walnuts, chopped
- 8 eggs
- 1 tsp baking powder
- 2 tsp vanilla
- 5 tbsp of granulated sweetener
- A pinch of salt

Directions

1. In a container, stir the butter, vanilla extract, and sweetener. A dash of salt, baking powder, coconut flour, and coffee should be added to the batter. Stir thoroughly. Mix thoroughly after adding each egg one at a time.

2. Combine the chopped walnuts with the rest of the ingredients. After pouring the batter into a baking dish that has been coated in baking paper, put the dish in an oven preheated to 356 degrees Fahrenheit for fifteen minutes. After it has cooled, cut it into 14 separate bars.

Nutrition

Calories: 150 | Fat: 11g | Carbs: 3g | Protein: 4g

DINNER

Protein-Rich Oatmeal

For persons weighing 77 kg and over, increase the ingredients by one-third.

Preparation Time: 4 Mins

Cooking Time: 1 Min

Servings: 2

Ingredients

- 1 scoop of whey protein powder
- 1 cup oatmeal
- ½ cup blueberries
- 2 tbsp raisins
- 2 tbsp pumpkin seeds
- ¼ cup of skim milk

Directions

1. In a bowl appropriate for the microwave, combine the protein powder and the oats.

2. Include some pumpkin seeds, some raisins, and some blueberries in the mix.

3. After that, pour in the milk, and allow the mixture to heat in the microwave for about a minute.

4. Mix thoroughly just before serving.

Nutrition

634 Calories | Protein 34g | Carbohydrates 55.7g | Fat 14.6g | Sodium 219.5mg

Ginger Sesame Pork Soup

For persons weighing 77 kg and over, increase the ingredients by one-third.

Preparation time: 10 Mins

Cooking time: 15 Mins

Servings: 2

Ingredients

- ½ tbsp avocado oil or extra-virgin olive oil
- 1 tsp sesame oil
- 8 oz ground pork
- 2 small carrots, diced
- 1-½ tsp minced peeled fresh ginger
- 4 cups chicken stock
- 2 tbsp soy sauce
- 1 cup halved sugar snap peas
- 1 cup thinly sliced Bok choy leaves
- Sea salt, as needed
- Freshly ground black pepper, as needed
- ½ jalapeño, seeded and thinly sliced
- ½ cup chopped fresh cilantro
- Juice of 1 lime

Directions

1. In a stockpot, heat both oils to medium-high heat. Cook the pork, carrots, and ginger in a saucepan, stirring constantly, for 5 to 7 mins, until either the pork is starting to brown.

2. The soy sauce and chicken stock should be added at this point. Bring the mixture to a boil.

3. The sugar snap peas should be cooked for ten mins, or until they reach the required tenderness, on a low heat with the lid on.

4. Add salt and pepper to taste once the bok choy leaves have been mixed.

5. Make two bowls and top each with chopped jalapeos, cilantro and lime juices.

Nutrition

Calories: 414 | Fat: 30g | Carbs: 14g | Protein: 23g

Curry and Grape Chicken Salad Lettuce Cups

For persons weighing 77 kg and over, increase the ingredients by one-third.

Preparation time: 15 Mins

Cooking time: 15 Mins

Servings: 2

Ingredients

- 1- 6 to 8 oz boneless chicken breast, cut into quarter-inch cubes
- ¼ cup mayonnaise
- 2 tbsp sour cream
- 2 tbsp halved red grapes
- 1 tbsp sliced almonds, toasted
- 1 tsp curry powder
- ¼ tsp sea salt
- ⅛ tsp ground white pepper
- 8 butter lettuce leaves

Directions:

1. In a standard size skillet or pot, combine the chicken with enough water to come halfway up the bird.

2. For 10 to 15 minutes until either the juices run clear, reduce the heat to medium-high and simmer the dish covered.

3. After removing the chicken from the poaching liquid, put it in the refrigerator for 15 to 20 minutes so that it may cool down.

4. Mix together the cooked and cooled chicken, along with the mayo, sour cream, the almonds, the curry powder, salt, and white pepper in a medium-sized bowl.

5. On the two plates, place 3 leaves of lettuce. The dish is ready to be served after dividing the chicken salad in a taco-style manner among the lettuce leaves.

Nutrition

Calories: 376 | Fat: 31g | Carbs: 4g | Protein: 19g

Celery Dill Soup

For persons weighing 77 kg and over, increase the ingredients by one-third.

Preparation Time: 5 Mins

Cooking Time: 25 Mins

Servings: 4

Ingredients

- 2 tbsp coconut oil
- ½ lb celery root, trimmed
- 1 garlic clove
- 1 medium white onion
- ¼ cup fresh dill, roughly chopped
- 1 tsp cumin powder
- ¼ tsp nutmeg powder
- 1 small head cauliflower, cut into florets
- 3-½ cups seasoned vegetable stock
- 5 oz vegan butter
- Juice from 1 lemon
- ¼ cup coconut cream
- Salt and black pepper to taste

Directions

1. To make the celery root, garlic, and onion soft and fragrant, heat the coconut oil in a large saucepan over medium heat.

2. Stir-frying the mixture for another minute after adding the dill, cumin, and nutmeg is recommended. Cauliflower and vegetable stock should be combined at this point. After 15 minutes of the soup being allowed to boil, the heat should be turned off.

3. After incorporating the vegan butter and the lemon juice into the soup, purée it with an immersion blender.

4. After incorporating the coconut cream, the soup is ready to be served after being seasoned with salt and black pepper. To be served hot.

Nutrition

Calories 320 | Fat 10 g | Protein 20 g | Carbohydrates 30 g

Orange & Kale Salad

For persons weighing 77 kg and over, increase the ingredients by one-third.

Preparation Time: 10 Mins

Cooking Time: 10 Mins

Servings: 2

Ingredients

For the Salad:

- 3 cups fresh kale, tough ribs removed and torn
- 2 oranges, peeled and segmented

- 2 tbsp fresh cranberries

For the Dressing:

- 2 tbsp olive oil

- 2 tbsp fresh orange juice

- ½ tsp agave nectar

- Sea salt, as needed

Directions:

For the salad:

1. Place all ingredients in a salad bowl and mix."

For the Dressing:

2. Place all ingredients in another bowl and beat until well combined.

3. Pour the dressing over the salad and coat. Serve immediately.

Nutrition

Calories 272 | Fats 2 g | Carbs 35.7 g | Protein 4.8 g

CHAPTER 11: Other Recipes

Breakfast Muffins

For persons weighing 77 kg and over, increase the ingredients by one-third.

Preparation Time: 10 Mins

Cooking Time: 30 Mins

Servings: 2

Ingredients

- 4 eggs
- 4 slices bacon, chopped and cooked
- ½ cup of almond flour
- ½ cup salsa

Directions

1. Turn the oven up to 350 degrees Fahrenheit. When oiling the muffin cups, it is preferable to use cooking spray rather than oiling them by hand.

2. In a blender, combine the eggs, bacon, almond flour, and salsa for thirty seconds on medium speed, or until everything is well combined, whichever comes first. Blend until smooth.

3. Fill muffin cups halfway with the mixture.

4. When a toothpick inserted into the centre of the muffin comes out clean, the muffin is done baking. 10 minutes of cooling time should be allowed before serving.

Nutrition

110 Calories | Protein 6.7g | Carbohydrates 2.9g | Fat 8.2g | Sodium 236.1mg

Quinoa Breakfast Bowl

For persons weighing 77 kg and over, increase the ingredients by one-third.

Preparation Time: 5 Mins

Cooking Time: 20 Mins

Servings: 1

Ingredients

- ¼ cup quinoa, multi-colored
- ½ cup of water
- ½ cup cottage cheese, reduced-sodium
- 1 tbsp fresh blueberries
- ½ sliced banana
- 1 pinch of ground cinnamon
- 1 tsp chia seeds

Directions

1. Bring water and quinoa to a boil in a saucepan. Use medium-low heat. Cover the pot and cook the quinoa for 15 to 20 minutes, depending on how soft you like your quinoa. After then, allow them to cool completely.

2. Mix half cup cottage cheese and quinoa in a bowl. Add on banana, chia seeds, cinnamon, and blueberries. Mix them well and serve.

Cook's Notes

• Other fruits, 1 to 2 tbsp low-sugar jam, nuts, and so on may be added.

• If you can buy it, use cottage cheese with no extra salt.

• Save any leftover quinoa for future snacks, salads, and breakfasts. Quinoa is a staple in many families since it is so adaptable.

Nutrition

313 Calories | Protein 21.1g | Carbohydrates 47.9g | Fat 4.7g | Sodium 21.6mg

Detox Fennel Smoothie

For persons weighing 77 kg and over, increase the ingredients by one-third.

Preparation Time: 5 Mins

Cooking Time: 0 Mins

Servings: 2

Ingredients

• 1 cup frozen pineapple

• 1 cup water or green tea

• 1 small fennel, chopped

• ½ cucumber, chopped

• 1 lime, peeled

Directions

1. Put the ingredients into a blender with a high-powered motor and process until smooth.

2. Serve, and have fun with it!

Nutrition

Calories: 276 | Carbs: 43g | Fat: 0g | Protein: 4g

Pomegranate and Fennel Smoothie

For persons weighing 77 kg and over, increase the ingredients by one-third.

Preparation Time: 5 Mins

Cooking Time: 0 Mins

Servings: 2

Ingredients

• 1 frozen banana

• 1 cup pomegranate juice

• 1 small fennel, chopped

• 1 pear, chopped

• 1 lime, juiced

Directions

1. Put the ingredients into a blender with a high-powered motor and process until smooth.

2. Serve, and have fun with it!

Nutrition

Calories: 283 | Carbs: 48g | Fat: 0g | Protein: 0g

Avocado Tuna Salad

For persons weighing 77 kg and over, increase the ingredients by one-third.

Preparation time: 15 Mins

Cooking time: 0 Mins

Servings: 6

Ingredients

• 3- 5 oz cans tuna, packed in water

- 2 large avocados, pitted, peeled, and chopped
- 2 large, hard-boiled eggs, chopped
- 3 tbsp mayonnaise
- 3 tbsp minced onion
- 2 tbsp minced celery
- ½ tsp of salt
- ¼ tsp freshly ground black pepper
- ⅛ teaspoon paprika

Directions

1. Put ingredients in a medium bowl and toss them together till they are evenly distributed.

2. Serve, and have fun with it!

3. **Nutrition**

4. Calories: 321 | Fat: 22 g | Protein: 23 g | Carbs: 6 g

Italian Fries

For persons weighing 77 kg and over, increase the ingredients by one-third.

Preparation Time: 15 Mins

Cooking Time: 40 Mins

Servings: 4

Ingredients

- ⅓ cup baby red potatoes

- 1 tbsp Italian seasoning
- 3 tbsp canola oil
- 1 tsp turmeric
- ½ tsp of sea salt
- ½ tsp dried rosemary
- 1 tbsp dried dill

Directions

1. Before putting them in the large bowl, cut the red potatoes into wedges. Add Italian spice, olive oil, turmeric, sea salt, dried rosemary and dill, and shake thoroughly.

2. Use baking paper to cover the bottom of your baking dish. Make sure the potato wedges are evenly distributed in the tray. The oven should be preheated to 375 degrees Fahrenheit before you begin baking.

3. Within 40 minutes, put the baking sheet in the oven and begin the baking process.. Make regular use of the spatula to mix the potatoes. Enjoy yourself while you're doing it!

Nutrition

Calories 152 | Fat 11.6g | Carbs 4.5g | Protein 0.6g

Kale Chips

For persons weighing 77 kg and over, increase the ingredients by one-third.

Preparation time: 5 Mins

Cooking time: 15 Mins

Servings: 2

Ingredients

- 7 oz kale
- 1 tbsp coconut oil

- 1 tsp chili powder
- 1 tsp cumin

Directions

1. The oven should be preheated to 400 degrees Fahrenheit. After rinsing, pat the kale dry. Tear the leaves into smaller pieces and throw away the stems.

2. Coat the kale with the coconut oil and spices by placing it in a mixing bowl and then tossing it.

3. Once the kale has been spread out in an even layer on the baking sheet, place the tray in the stove and cook it for fifteen minutes, or until the kale is browned and crispy, whichever comes first. Immediately serve after cooking.

Nutrition

Calories: 150 | Carbs: 18g | Fat: 6g | Protein: 3g

Sweet Potato Chips

For persons weighing 77 kg and over, increase the ingredients by one-third.

Preparation Time: 15 Mins

Cooking Time: 60 Mins

Servings: 2

Ingredients

- "1 large sweet potato"
- "1 tbsp extra-virgin olive oil"
- "Salt, as needed"

Directions

1. Pre-heat the kiln to 300°F. Make your potato look like french fries by cutting it into small slices.

2. Salt and extra-virgin olive oil should be tossed with the potato pieces that have been placed in a mixing bowl. Bake for one hour, turning the potatoes over once every 15 minutes, until they are crisp and golden brown.

Nutrition

Calories: 150 | Carbs: 16g | Fat: 9g | Protein: 1g

Pita Chips

For persons weighing 77 kg and over, increase the ingredients by one-third.

Preparation Time: 15 Mins

Cooking Time: 10 Mins

Servings: 1 cup

Ingredients

- 3 pitas
- ¼ cup extra-virgin olive oil
- ¼ cup za'atar

Directions

1. Turn the oven up to 450 degrees Fahrenheit. Each pita should be sliced into pieces that are roughly 2 inches long, and then those pieces should be arranged in the large bowl.

2. After drizzling pitas using extra-virgin olive oil and sprinkling them with za'atar, they should be tossed so the oil and spice mixture is distributed evenly throughout the pitas.

3. It is recommended that pitas be roasted on a baking pan for approximately 8 to 10 mins,

or till they have a colour that is similar to a light golden brown.

4. Before attempting to remove it off the baking sheet, you should first let it cool completely. While you're at it, have some fun!

Nutrition

Calories: 158 | Carbs: 18 g | Fat: 2 g | Protein: 5 g"

Loaded Barbecue Roasted Cabbage Steaks

For persons weighing 77 kg and over, increase the ingredients by one-third.

Preparation time: 10 Mins

Cooking time: 35 Mins

Servings: 2

Ingredients

- ½ head cabbage, sliced into 4 (1-inch-thick) steaks
- 2 tbsp avocado oil
- 1 tsp freshly ground black pepper
- ½ tsp sea salt
- 2 tbsp sugar-free barbecue sauce
- 1 avocado, diced
- ½ jalapeño, seeded and thinly sliced
- 1 scallion, chopped
- 2 tbsp sour cream
- ½ cup chopped fresh cilantro

Directions

1. Put a cooking pan in the kiln and turn the temperature up to 400 degrees Fahrenheit. Prepare a baking sheet by lining it with parchment paper.

2. The cabbage steaks should be seasoned with pepper and salt, and then a drizzle of oil should be drizzled across both sides of the cabbage steaks.

3. After 15 minutes in the oven, turn the meat over and continue roasting for another 15 minutes after that. The cabbage should be browned with a tender center. Remove the cabbage steaks and turn the oven to broil.

4. Dividing evenly, top each cabbage steak with the barbecue sauce. Broil for 3 to 5 minutes.

5. On each serving plate, arrange two steaks, then top them with avocado, jalapeo, onion, and cilantro, and finish with sour cream.

Nutrition

Calories: 493 | Fat: 41g | Carbs: 24g | Protein: 13g

Steak Bites and Zucchini Noodles

For persons weighing 77 kg and over, increase the ingredients by one-third.

Preparation time: 15 minutes

Cooking time: 15 minutes

Servings: 2

Ingredients

- 3 tbsp olive oil
- 4 garlic cloves, peeled and minced
- 1 tbsp soy sauce
- ½ tsp garlic powder
- ½ tbsp paprika
- ½ teaspoon black pepper
- 18 oz sirloin steak, diced
- 3 zucchinis, spiralized

Directions

1. When the olive oil has reached a temperature of around two tablespoons, include the garlic to the cooking pan. Cook for a total of 5 minutes till the scent is released.

2. To ensure that the soy sauce, garlic powder, paprika, and black pepper are uniformly distributed, mix all of the ingredients together. Put to the side to cool while you work on the remaining components of the dish.

3. The skillet should be heated with one tablespoon of olive oil before adding the meat that has been diced. Continue to cook the steak until it reaches an almost-done state.

4. After pouring the sauce into the pan, continue cooking the steak for one more minute while stirring it to ensure that it is completely covered in the sauce.

5. If desired, heat the zucchini noodles or serve them cold alongside the steak bites.

Nutrition:

Calories: 331 |Carbs 9g | Protein 20g | Fat 8g

Beef Burger on a Mushroom Bun

For persons weighing 77 kg and over, increase the ingredients by one-third.

Preparation time: 15 Mins

Cooking time: 10 Mins

Servings: 2

Ingredients

- 14 oz minced beef
- 1 tsp paprika
- 2 tbsp BBQ sauce
- 2 tbsp olive oil
- 4 large mushrooms
- 1 onion, sliced
- 4 cherry tomatoes, sliced
- Handful lettuce
- 1 avocado, peeled and sliced

Directions

1. Combine the ground beef, smoked paprika, and barbecue sauce in a bowl and set aside. Form the ingredients into four equal burger patties.

2. To begin, heat one tbsp of olive oil in a big skillet over medium heat. Once the oil is hot, add the mushrooms and cook them for five minutes on each side, or until they are crisp and have developed a light brown colour.

3. Continue cooking the vegetables with the one tbsp of olive oil that is left in the pan after the mushrooms have been removed.

4. Add the beef patties as well as the onion. Cook for approximately four to five minutes on

each side, or until the beef has tanned and the onions have become transparent.

5. Create your burgers by placing the mushrooms on a plate and topping each with a beef burger, cherry tomatoes, lettuce, and avocado slices.

6. Add some more BBQ sauce and paprika for extra flavor. Serve, and have fun with it!

Nutrition

Calories 498 | Carbs 6g | Protein 31g | Fat 22g

Teriyaki Chicken and Broccoli

For persons weighing 77 kg and over, increase the ingredients by one-third.

Preparation time: 15 Mins

Cooking time: 13-15 Mins

Servings: 2

Ingredients

- ¼ cup coconut aminos
- 2 tbsp granulated erythritol
- 2 tbsp rice vinegar
- 1 tbsp sesame oil
- 1 tbsp fresh grated ginger
- 2 cloves garlic, minced
- ⅛ tsp crushed red pepper flakes
- ½ teaspoon arrowroot powder
- 2 tbsp fresh orange juice
- 2 tbsp olive oil
- 1-½ lb chicken breasts, boneless, skinless, cubed
- 1 teaspoon salt
- ½ teaspoon freshly ground black pepper
- ½ teaspoon garlic powder
- 2 cups broccoli florets
- 2 tbsp sesame seeds

Directions

1. Melt coconut aminos with erythritol and orange juice in a saucepan with the rest of the ingredients. Don't let it boil.

2. Continue to whisk the mixture as it boils for two to three minutes, or until the consistency of the sauce alters, whichever comes first. After then, remove the pan from the fire and allow it to come to room temperature.

3. In a skillet of mid sized and over medium-high heat, olive oil should be brought up to temperature. After adding the chicken cubes and waiting approximately 7 minutes, check to see if the chicken is cooked all the way through before seasoning it with salt, pepper, and garlic powder.

4. Pour prepared teriyaki sauce over the chicken. Allow coming to a slight boil.

5. Toss the broccoli florets in the sauce until they are well coated. Keep the lid on the saucepan and let the broccoli cook for about three mins, or till it reaches the desired degree of tenderness. Serve, and don't forget to have fun doing it!

Nutrition:

Calories: 240 | Fat: 11g | Protein: 27g | Carbs: 10g

Ground Beef Hash

Preparation time: 15 Mins

Cooking time: 15-20 Mins

Servings: 6

Ingredients

- 4 tbsp avocado oil
- 2 cups roughly chopped cauliflower
- ¼ cup chopped yellow onion
- 1 tbsp minced jalapeño
- 1-½ lb ground beef
- 1 tsp granulated garlic
- 1 tsp granulated onion
- 1 tsp salt
- 1 tsp freshly ground black pepper
- ½ tsp dried parsley

Directions

1. Warm the avocado oil in the medium skillet by placing it over high heat. After the oil has reached the desired temperature, add the cauliflower.

2. After giving the cauliflower a single stir to coat it, set it aside for 2 minutes without stirring it, and keep a close eye on it to ensure it doesn't burn. After another stir, let the cauliflower remain for an additional 2 minutes.

3. The onions and jalapenos should be added to the pan once the temperature has been reduced to medium.Cook for about four mins, or till it has become more malleable, until it has become more malleable.

4. Continue to cook the beef for approximately seven minutes after you have added the spices and herbs, or till the meat is not anymore pink in the centre. Then remove it from the heat, and serve it to the guests!

Nutrition:

Calories: 427 | Fat: 31 g | Protein: 31 g | Carbs: 4 g

Herb and Lemon Roasted Vegetables

For persons weighing 77 kg and over, increase the ingredients by one-third.

Preparation time: 10 Mins

Cooking time: 35 Mins

Servings: 2

Ingredients

- 8 brussels sprouts, quartered
- 8 baby Bella (cremini) mushrooms
- 1 medium carrot, cut into quarter-inch pieces
- 1 red bell pepper, cut into half-inch-wide strips
- 1 head broccoli, cut into small florets
- ½ red onion, cut into half-inch pieces
- 8 garlic cloves, peeled
- 2 tbsp avocado oil
- 1 tsp freshly ground black pepper
- ½ tsp sea salt
- ½ cup halved cherry tomatoes
- 1 tbsp fresh thyme
- 2 tsp chopped fresh oregano
- ½ lemon

Directions

1. Preheat the oven to 400°F. Prepare a sheet of parchment paper to line your baking sheet.

2. On the baking sheet that has been prepped, combine the brussels sprouts, mushrooms, carrots, bell peppers, broccoli, onion, and garlic together. Bake for 30 minutes.

3. The oil should be drizzled over the vegetables after the black pepper and salt have been added. The vegetables should then be gently tossed so that they are coated with the oil and the seasonings. Roast them for around 15 to 20 minutes, or until they start to get soft.

4. Toss the tomatoes, thyme, and oregano that have been added to the baking sheet before placing it in the oven to brown the veggies.

Nutrition:

Calories: 349 | Fat: 16g | Carbs: 45g | Protein: 15g

Jambalaya Squash Ribbons

For persons weighing 77 kg and over, increase the ingredients by one-third.

Preparation time: 25 Mins

Cooking time: 20 Mins

Servings: 2

Ingredients

- 2 tbsp unsalted butter
- 1 small yellow onion, sliced into half-moons
- 2 medium yellow squash, thinly sliced
- 1 medium zucchini, thinly sliced
- 1 medium carrot, peeled and julienned
- 1 medium red bell pepper, seeded & julienned
- 1medium green bell pepper, seeded & julienned
- 1 medium tomato, diced
- 1 cup raw edamame, shelled
- 1 tbsp minced garlic
- 1 tbsp Cajun seasoning
- ½ cup dry white wine
- 3 cups vegetable stock
- ¼ cup chopped fresh flat-leaf parsley

Directions

1. Place the large skillet you have on top of the burner, and raise the temperature to its highest setting. Keep heating up the skillet until it starts to give off smoke.

2. After adding the butter and allowing it to melt, continue by adding the remaining ingredients, which are as follows: onion, yellow squash, zucchini, carrot, red and green bell peppers, tomato, edamame, garlic, Cajun seasoning, as well as a sprinkle of salt and pepper.

3. Cook the vegetables at a heat setting of medium, stirring them frequently, for around six minutes, or until they have taken on some colour.

4. First, the pan should be deglazed with the wine, and then the stock should be added. After adding the parsley, go on with the cooking for another five to ten minutes, or until the liquid has evaporated to about a

quarter of its original volume. To be consumed while heated.

Nutrition:

Calories: 255 | Fat: 11g | Carbs: 26g | Protein: 13g

Chicken Kale Wraps

For persons weighing 77 kg and over, increase the ingredients by one-third.

Preparation Time: 15 Mins

Cooking Time: 10 Mins

Servings: 2

Ingredients

- 4 kale leaves
- 4 oz chicken fillet
- ½ apple
- 1 tbsp butter
- ¼ tsp chili pepper
- ¾ tsp salt
- 1 tbsp lemon juice
- ¾ tsp dried thyme

Directions

1. Using a sharp knife, cut the chicken tenderloin into pieces that are suitable for nibbling. Salt and chile pepper should be mixed into the chicken that has been placed in a mixing bowl. Butter should be melted in the pan, then chicken cubes should be added. They should be roasted in the next 4 minutes.

2. While that is going on, dice up your apple into little pieces. It is then sprinkled with lemon juice and dried thyme before being added to the chicken.

3. They need to be cooked for five mins over a heat setting that is considered to be medium. After the kale leaves have been packed with the chicken mixture, wrap the stuffed kale leaves with the chicken mixture.

Nutrition:

Calories: 370 | Carbs: 34g | Fat: 14g | Protein: 29g

Pork Belly Bombs

For persons weighing 77 kg and over, increase the ingredients by one-third.

Preparation Time: 15 Mins

Cooking Time: 40 Mins

Servings: 2

Ingredients

- ¼ cup mayonnaise
- 7 oz pork belly, cooked
- 3 bacon slices, cut in half
- 1 tbsp horseradish, fresh & grated
- 1 tbsp Dijon mustard
- 6 lettuce leaves for serving
- Sea salt & black pepper to taste

Directions

1. First, preheat your oven to 320°F, then cook your bacon for 30 minutes at that temperature. After you've given it some time to cool, crumble your bacon. Put it in a bowl or plate.

2. To prepare, shred the pork belly and place it in a basin. Mix in your horseradish, mayonnaise, and mustard into the dish. Combine it, and then season it.

3. Divide this mixture into six mounds and roll it in your crumbled bacon. Serve on lettuce leaves.

Nutrition:

Calories 153 | Protein 3.5g | Fat 26.4g | Carbs 0.3g

Slow-Cooked Cajun Boiled Peanuts

For persons weighing 77 kg and over, increase the ingredients by one-third.

Preparation time: 5 Mins

Cooking time: 12 Hrs

Servings: 2

Ingredients

- 6 cups raw peanuts in the shell
- 2- 12 oz bottles or cans of low-carb beer
- 4 cups of water
- 2 tbsp Cajun seasoning
- 4 bay leaves

Directions

1. Put the peanuts, beer, water, Cajun seasoning, and bay leaves into the slow cooker and mix everything together. Cook for a maximum of 12 hours on high with the lid on.

2. Remove any excess liquid from the peanuts, then set them aside to cool for 10 minutes. As you munch, enjoy the peanuts and toss the shells; then, place any leftovers in a jar that seals tightly and stores them in the fridge.

Nutrition:

Calories: 153 | Fat: 14g | Carbs: 3g | Protein: 7g

Tomatoes deviled egg

For persons weighing 77 kg and over, increase the ingredients by one-third.

Preparation time: 15 Mins

Cooking time: 0 Mins

Servings: 2

Ingredients

- 6 large hardboiled eggs, peeled and roughly chopped
- ¼ cup chopped celery
- ¼ cup chopped fresh chives, plus more to garnish
- 2 tbsp mayonnaise
- 2 tsp Creole or grainy mustard
- 4 dashes of hot sauce
- 1 tsp barbecue dry rub seasoning
- ¼ tsp kosher salt
- ½ tsp cracked black pepper
- 6 small Roma tomatoes
- ½ cup thinly sliced purple cabbage

Directions

1. Collect the items you will need for the omelettes in a large bowl, and then combine them with the mayonnaise, mustard, and hot sauce, along with the dry barbecue rub, salt, and pepper.

2. Put the tomatoes in the refrigerator while you prepare them.

3. After slicing each Roma tomato in ½ lengthwise, use a spoon to remove the seeds and flesh from the tomato.

4. Scoop 1 to 2 tablespoons of the egg mixture into each tomato half. Garnish with chives and slices of purple cabbage.

Nutrition:

Calories: 152 | Fat: 11g | Carbs: 9g | Protein: 11g

Chocolate Haystacks

For persons weighing 77 kg and over, increase the ingredients by one-third.

Preparation time: 20 Mins

Cooking time: 5 Mins

Servings: 2

Ingredients

- 6 oz Stevia-sweetened chocolate
- 2 tbsp coconut oil
- 3 tbsp Swerve confectioners
- 1 cup shredded unsweetened coconut (or flakes or a combination)
- 1 cup coarsely chopped pecans

Directions

1. Use parchment paper to cover a baking sheet.

2. Place a bowl made of glass or metal on top of a pot containing boiling water, and then add the chocolate and the coconut oil to the bowl. After the chocolate has melted, remove the pan from the heat.

3. Cook the mixture while stirring it frequently until the Swerve has been completely incorporated. Reduce the temperature by one or two notches. To the mixture, add the shredded coconut and chopped pecans.

4. Place spoonfuls of the batter onto the prepared baking sheet. Place the mixture in the refrigerator for at least two hours, or until it has completely solidified.

Nutrition:

Calories: 152 | Fat: 16g | Carbs: 4g | Protein: 5g

High-Protein Nutty Pasta

For persons weighing 77 kg and over, increase the ingredients by one-third.

Preparation Time: 15 Mins

Cooking Time: 20 Mins

Servings: 2

Ingredients

- "1- 8 oz package quinoa pasta"
- 1 drizzle of olive oil, extra-virgin
- ¼ cup tofu, diced
- 2 tbsp grated cheese blend, Parmesan & Romano
- 2 tbsp feta cheese, crumbled
- "2 tbsp chopped pecans"
- "2 tbsp sunflower seeds, roasted"
- "2 tbsp slivered or sliced almonds"
- ½ tsp dried parsley
- 2 tbsp pimentos, minced
- "Pepper and salt according to taste"
- 1 tbsp butter

Directions

1. Bring a large saucepan of water to a rolling boil, and season liberally with salt. Before serving, stir in the extra virgin olive oil and the quinoa pasta.

2. A few minutes later, add the pasta and continue cooking for an additional 13 to 15 minutes. Set aside the spaghetti after it has been drained.

3. Feta cheese, tofu, Parmesan & Romano cheese and almonds, pecans, sunflower seeds, and parsley are all mixed together in a large salad dish.

4. Stir the melted butter into the hot spaghetti to incorporate everything.

Nutrition:

347 Calories | Protein 10.8g | Carbohydrates 45.4g | Fat 13.6g | Sodium 147mg

Eggs and Greens Dish

For persons weighing 77 kg and over, increase the ingredients by one-third.

Preparation Time: 10 Mins

Cooking Time: 10 Mins

Servings: 2

Ingredients

- 1 tbsp olive oil
- 1 cup of fresh spinach
- 2 cups of chopped and stemmed rainbow chard
- Ground black pepper and salt to taste
- ½ cup of arugula
- 4 eggs, beaten
- 2 minced cloves of garlic
- ½ cup of shredded cheddar cheese

Directions

1. The oil should be simmering in a medium-sized skillet.

2. After 3 minutes of cooking, the spinach, arugula, and chard should be soft. Continue cooking and stirring for 2 minutes after adding the garlic.

3. Toss the chard mix with the cheese-egg mixture, and stir thoroughly.

4. It should be ready in 5 to 7 minutes after you apply the coating, or when it's set. Spice things up by adding salt and pepper to your dish as needed.

Nutrition:

333 Calories | Protein 21g | Carbohydrates 4.2g | Fat 26.2g | Sodium 483.5mg

Clam Chowder

For persons weighing 77 kg and over, increase the ingredients by one-third.

Preparation Time: 5 Mins

Cooking Time: 40 Mins

Servings: 2

Ingredients

- 1-½ cups of garbanzo beans cooked
- 1-½ cups of chopped oyster mushrooms
- 2 cups of garbanzo bean flour
- 1 cup of mashed white onions
- ½ cup of chopped butternut squash
- ½ cup of medium diced kale
- 1 cup of homemade hemp seed milk
- 1 cup of Aquafaba
- 2 teaspoons of dill"
- ½ teaspoon of cayenne powder
- 2 teaspoons of basil
- 1 tbsp of pure sea salt

- 1 tbsp of grape seed oil
- 7 cups of water

Directions

1. Add 6 cups of spring water and Aquafaba to a big pot and bring to a boil.

2. Pour half of each seasoning mix into the pot with the cooked garbanzo beans and chopped vegetables.

3. Bring to a boil, then simmer, stirring periodically for 10 minutes.

4. In a separate bowl, combine the hempseed milk, grape seed oil, 1 cup of spring water, and the remaining seasonings. The chickpea flour should be whisked in gradually.

5. When the mixture is smooth and free of lumps, add the flour one tablespoon at a time.

6. To avoid lumps, slowly pour in the ingredients while whisking.

7. Cook the oyster mushrooms for 10 minutes on a low heat setting. Every now and again, stir the soup.

8. Dish out your vegan clam chowder and savor it!

Nutrition:

Calories: 127 | Fat: 3.5g | Carbs: 3.6g | Protein: 21.5g | Fiber: 0.4g

American Pancakes

For persons weighing 77 kg and over, increase the ingredients by one-third.

Preparation Time: 10 Mins

Cooking Time: 10 Mins

Servings: 2

Ingredients

- 1 ripe banana, cut into pieces
- 1 tbsp chia seeds
- 2 eggs
- ½ teaspoon dark cocoa powder (optional)
- 1 tbsp all-purpose flour
- ½ teaspoon ground cinnamon (optional)
- 1 pinch of sea salt
- ½ teaspoon vanilla extract (optional)
- ¼ cup of blueberries
- 1 tbsp coconut oil or more as required

Directions

1. Add chia seeds to a blender. Blend them until powdery for 3 to 5 seconds. Add eggs, banana, flour, cinnamon, cocoa powder, sea salt, and vanilla extract; blend, usually scraping sides, until the batter is uniform and smooth.

2. Heat a skillet to a medium-high temperature. Heat the coconut oil in a large skillet over medium heat. Pour half of the batter into the oil. Add half of the blueberries to the batter.

3. Then cook it until the bubbles are formed, and the edges are dried for about 3 to 4 minutes.

4. Cook them while flipping until browned on both sides, for 2 to 3minutes. Repeat with the leftover blueberries and batter by using coconut oil if required.

Nutrition:

233 Calories | Protein 8.2g | Carbohydrates 22g | Fat 13.5g | Sodium 231.8mg

Banana Bread

For persons weighing 77 kg and over, increase the ingredients by one-third.

Preparation Time: 10 Mins

Cooking Time: 2 Hrs 30 Mins

Servings: 2

Ingredients

- 1-¼ cups of oat flour
- 1 serving cooking spray, nonstick
- ½ cup of white sugar
- 2 scoops of chocolate protein powder
- ½ cup walnuts, chopped
- 3 teaspoon ground cinnamon
- ½ teaspoon baking soda
- 1-½ teaspoon baking powder
- 3 overripe and mashed bananas
- ¼ cup milk
- ½ cup applesauce, unsweetened
- 3 tsp pure vanilla extract
- 2egg whites, large

Directions

1. Set the oven temperature to 350°F. Spray a 9-by-5-inch loaf pan with cooking spray.

2. A medium mixing bowl is a perfect place for combining the dry ingredients. Add in the wet ingredients and stir until well combined.

3. Combine applesauce, mashed bananas, milk, vanilla extract, and egg whites in a large mixing dish. Take care not to over-mix the banana mixture as you gradually add in the flour mixture. Finally, incorporate the prepared batter into the loaf pan.

4. When a toothpick pushed into the bread comes out clean, the bread is done baking. For 10 minutes, leave the baked products in the pan. Before serving, allow to cool entirely on a wire rack.

Nutrition:

193 Calories | Protein 6.9g | Carbohydrates 31g | Fat 5.4g | Sodium 187.1mg

Eggs Florentine

For persons weighing 77 kg and over, increase the ingredients by one-third.

Preparation Time: 10 Mins

Cooking Time: 10 Mins

Servings: 2

Ingredients

- 2 tbsp butter
- 2 minced cloves of garlic
- 3 tbsp cream cheese, diced into small pieces
- ½ cup of mushrooms, diced
- ½- 10 oz package of fresh spinach
- Ground black pepper and salt according to taste
- 6 large eggs, beaten slightly

Directions

1. Garlic and mushrooms should be cooked in butter in a large skillet over medium heat for about one minute, stirring constantly to prevent burning.

2. Add the spinach to the mushroom mixture and cook for 2 to 3 minutes, or until the spinach has wilted.

3. Add the eggs and season with salt and pepper to the mushroom-spinach combination.

4. Flip the eggs after they've boiled for a few minutes.

5. Cook for 5 minutes, stirring occasionally, after adding the cream cheese to the egg mixture.

Nutrition:

279 Calories | Protein 15.7g | Carbohydrates 4.1g | Fat 22.9g | Sodium 276mg

Zucchini with Egg

For persons weighing 77 kg and over, increase the ingredients by one-third.

Preparation Time: 5 Mins

Cooking Time: 15 Mins

Servings: 2

Ingredients

- 1-½ tbsp olive oil
- Ground black pepper and salt to taste
- 2 zucchinis, large, diced into large chunks
- 1 tsp water, or as required
- 2 large eggs

Directions

1. After heating the oil in a skillet over a medium-high flame, sauté the zucchini for about 10 minutes, or until it reaches the desired tenderness. Add some freshly ground black pepper and salt to the zucchini.

2. In a bowl, whisk the eggs with a fork, then add the water and continue to whisk until everything is thoroughly blended. After pouring the eggs over the zucchini, continue to cook the mixture while stirring for approximately 5 minutes, or until the eggs have become scrambled and are no longer runny. Salt and black pepper should be sprinkled on the eggs and zucchini.

Nutrition:

213 Calories | Protein 10.2g | Carbohydrates 11.2g | Fat 15.7g | Sodium 180mg

Caprese On Toast

For persons weighing 77 kg and over, increase the ingredients by one-third.

Preparation Time: 15 Mins

Cooking Time: 5 Mins

Servings: 2

Ingredients

- 14 slices of sourdough bread
- 1 lb fresh mozzarella cheese, diced quarter-inch thick
- 2 peeled cloves of garlic
- ⅓ cup of fresh basil leaves
- 3 tbsp extra-virgin olive oil
- 3 large tomatoes, diced quarter-inch thick
- Ground black pepper and salt to taste

Directions

1. After the bread pieces have been toasted, massage the garlic cloves on both sides of each slice.

2. On top of each piece of bread, layer one slice of tomato, one slice of mozzarella cheese, and one to two basil leaves. After that, finish it with a drizzle of olive oil and season it with pepper and salt.

Nutrition:

204 Calories | Protein 10.5g | Carbohydrates 16.5g | Fat 10.7g | Sodium 368mg

Quinoa Cereal

For persons weighing 77 kg and over, increase the ingredients by one-third.

Preparation Time: 5 Mins

Cooking Time: 16 Mins

Servings: 2

Ingredients

- 1 cup of quinoa, rinsed
- 1 tsp ground cinnamon
- 2 cups of water
- ½ cup of dried apricots, chopped
- ⅓ cup of flax seeds
- ½ cup of slivered almonds
- ½ teaspoon ground nutmeg

Directions

1. In a saucepan set over a medium flame, combine the water and quinoa, and then bring the mixture to a boil. Reduce the heat and continue boiling for 8 to 12 minutes, or until most of the water has been absorbed.

2. Mix in almonds, apricots, flax seeds, nutmeg, and cinnamon; cook till the quinoa is tender for 2 to 3 minutes more.

Nutrition:

350 Calories | Protein 11.8g | Carbohydrates 44.5g | Fat 15.1g | Sodium 12.8mg

Conclusion

At the conclusion of Whole Body Reset Diet book, here are a few more thoughts about the diet in general. One thing about this way of eating is that it's very flexible. If you want to eat some carbs one day but not another, you can do that much more easily than when following most other diets. Of course, this is not always recommended. But you can feel more at ease with the dietary requirements of Whole Body Reset Diet.

The same goes for eating more in some meals and less in others. Because all foods are acceptable in moderation, you can adjust your portions throughout the day as your cravings, and hunger level dictates. When it comes to losing weight, this is a huge plus. You can eat a little more of a particular food group if you want, but it will be eaten in moderation. As a result, you won't feel deprived or crave an unhealthy second helping of anything.

Another good thing about Whole Body Reset Diet is that it's very flexible for most people. It doesn't include some restrictive dietary plans out there, and it also doesn't require weighing and measuring every bite you take to ensure your portions. As a result, it's a relatively easy way to eat if you're looking to live a healthier lifestyle. It does take a little planning and preparation, but that's the nature of most diets. In this case, the diet is worthwhile because it keeps your cravings at bay and helps you lose weight more sustainably.

As mentioned above, this diet is geared toward people looking to live healthier lives rather than just losing weight. It's great for losing weight, but it also recommends many healthy habits that are meant to be practiced long after you reach your goal weight. Keeping the body healthy is essential to maintaining a healthy weight, and that's why it's most definitely a diet worth considering.

If you are looking for some specific recipes to use while on Whole Body Reset Diet, check out the detailed recipe section of this book. It contains many solid options to get you started!

Made in the USA
Las Vegas, NV
14 November 2023

80831816R00061